KIDS NAVIGATING LIFE

Level 3

Sue Mackey with
Laura Tonkin & Rachael Ashbaugh

Book Publishers Network
P.O. Box 2256
Bothell • WA • 98041
PH • 425-483-3040
www.bookpublishersnetwork.com

Copyright © 2008 by The Mackey Group
Graphic clipart © 2008 Jupiterimages Corporation

All rights reserved. No part of this book may be reproduced, stored in, or introduced into a retrieval system, or transmitted in any form, or by any means (electronic, mechanical, photocopying, recording, or otherwise) without the prior written permission of the publisher.

10 9 8 7 6 5 4 3 2 1

Printed in the United States of America

    LCCN 2008928365
    ISBN10 1-887542-80-9
    ISBN13 978-1-887542-80-7

Editor: Tracy Musgrow
Cover Designer: Amanda Predmore
Typographer: Stephanie Martindale

Contents

Foreword v

Introduction vii

Trainer's Manual ix

Communicating Effectively 1

Dealing with Emotions 15

Building Character 33

Thinking Critically 49

Gaining Social Skills 67

Planning a Project 81

Making a Difference 97

Kids Navigating Life - Level 3

Foreword

As I read, *Kids Navigating Life*, I couldn't help but think that there has never been a time in the history of education that materials like this are more needed. *Kids Navigating Life,* is a **must have** for every classroom, home, and young person. This is perhaps the most influential teaching and learning tool that has been developed in all my twenty-seven years of teaching.

As a former teacher, I can attest to the value of teaching our youth sustainable life (soft) skills. From my perspective, to only teach the basic academic subjects and think children are completely prepared to function well and appropriately in society is impractical. They must have life skills because they are fundamental to a child's success in school and later in their adult life. Unfortunately, life skills have not been a focus of academia until The Mackey Group published the *Living Well, Working Smart: Soft Skills for Success* book which has provided a standard for learning and utilizing these skills effectively. Now available, another much needed yet simplified version for our youth.

As an internationally recognized speaker and lecturer on attitude, confidence, and success, I teach how to attain and sustain success in whatever you choose to do, the core competencies, the soft skills required to succeed are not an option but a necessity. Knowing how to use these skills effectively enables adults and our children to not only know what to do but to know how to do it well, in any situation.

Kids Navigating Life will be a vital tool in the development of our children's lives for years to come. There is nothing like this -- an extraordinary piece of work that is long overdue.

DeLores Pressley
Former Educator
International Speaker and Author
Principal, BornSuccessful Consultants
www.bornsuccessful.com

Introduction

Whether we're a parent, teacher, counselor, or mentor of young people, our job is teaching and training. Our responsibility to our youth is to educate and inform, to teach and to demonstrate, and to transform kids from being reactionary to being fully self-directed and guided by a strong, internal compass. Having that compass will mean the difference between success and failure. It will help them navigate life, its challenges and opportunities, more productively, responsibly and, too, will guide them into being productive members of society. *Kids Navigating Life* is the foundation, the development tool for navigating life with a reliable, trustworthy compass.

Kids Navigating Life was conceived during my many interviews for *Women Navigating Adversity: The Courage They Didn't Know They Had.* It's a book profiling a dozen everyday women and how they managed or overcame adversity in their lives. Many expressed how invaluable it would have been had they had the life skill knowledge and training when they were growing up. They would have been able to avoid or deal with life's unexpected and unwelcomed events faster and better. And too, some acknowledged that they wouldn't have made some of the choices they did had they had a better understanding of how to make good decisions and how to problem solve effectively. Good relationships were a primary key to overcoming their challenges, yet few had the skill knowledge necessary to understand how to develop these relationships and use them as resources.

While many of these women have a college education, they admitted that their academic learning did little to prepare them for real life. In fact, many stated their educations taught them what they needed to know to get a job but failed in teaching them how to succeed in their jobs. Many, too, expressed their frustration at knowing **what** to do but not **how** to do it well.

Hearing this, and not for the first time, we embarked on a mission to put our years of expertise in the development of skill standards, hard (technical) and soft (life) skills, to work for kids. Our book, *Living Well, Working Smart: The Soft Skills for Success* sets the standard for 41 life skills and has now been adapted for children. If we could give our young people an early start in life to learn what so many adults wished they had been taught; imagine the advantage they'd have in life. The positive impact on our youth would make a significant difference in their lives, now and with each passing year of their life.

What has been of paramount importance to us in the development process was making sure that each learner would complete his/her workbook and realize that he/she not only knew what to do but knew how to do it well. Simply telling children what it is they need to do in a scenario is not enough. If the scenario doesn't play out as explained – few ever do – the children will make poor choices. They won't know what to do nor will they know how to do it well. But if the learner is taught what to do with each skill and taught how to use it in any given situation or with any scenario, they will have learned for a lifetime of use the

Kids Navigating Life - Level 3

effectiveness of each skill. Throughout their lives they will continue to become more proficient in the use of each skill as life experiences are accrued.

A good example of the difference between what and how would be telling a child to have a positive attitude. While this may appear to be a simple request, if the child fails to know what other skills are required to sustain a positive attitude, he or she won't. If the child hasn't been taught good decision making skills or problem solving skills or doesn't know that it takes a host of skills to make good decisions or to problem solve effectively, develop good relationships with peers and adults, a positive attitude cannot be sustained.

The same applies for any task. Employers are searching for employees who not only know what to do but who know how to do it well, which is life skill dependent, or in the vernacular of the corporate world, have the core competencies required to perform well. Universities throughout the country, Harvard included, have begun developing curriculum for teaching life skills, the core competencies, in their business schools. They are responding to the needs of employers requiring more than just graduates knowing what to do.

By you introducing and teaching these vital skills to our young people, you are giving them a life long advantage. You are helping them develop an internal life compass to help guide their way to successful living. They will be able to manage their lives far more effectively, regardless of the circumstances. They will make better choices and decisions. And, too, they will be able to succeed in whatever they do with the knowledge of and implementation of these vital skills in all that they do.

You will have left a legacy of extraordinary value to each individual and to our society as a whole. It's a gift that will touch one first and then untold numbers of people throughout the life of that one individual.

Trainer's Manual

Every child is unique and develops at his or her own pace. Many factors affect and influence each child's abilities: from family involvement, school environment, social comfort, background, tolerance level, expectations, and temperament, just to name a few.

Because all children have varying abilities, the Kids Navigating Life courseware is written in several skill levels to accommodate each student's unique stage of education. It is important to choose the appropriate level for your student, as the activities in each section correlate with age-specific developmental milestones.

The goal of each workbook is to teach the life skills and strategies that will show kids how to successfully navigate life. Life skills and how kids use them will determine the quality of their lives.

Life skills are very important to our children's futures. They can't succeed without these skills. They are part of everything children do, and they use them every day. How children demonstrate or apply life skills is critical to the outcome of what they want to achieve.

The Kids Navigating Life courseware is outcome driven. Outcome driven courseware promotes higher expectations by asking students to demonstrate what they know and have learned. This can be demonstrated in many ways such as producing a product (e.g., drawing), a service (e.g., presentation, doing something for someone), or making a decision based on the information gathered.

Outcome driven courseware also allows the [1]trainer to effectively assess students' level of knowledge and their application of the skill. A student may produce a drawing according to written instructions thereby demonstrating the student can follow written instructions.

By the time students finish the exercises in this workbook, they will understand why some people manage life well and others have difficulty. They will also discover a lot about themselves. It will be clear which skills they need to work on and which ones they are already good at. But most importantly, they will discover they can succeed in what they choose to do with what they've learned. The mysteries about why some people succeed and others don't will become very clear.

How To Use The Workbooks

The workbooks are designed for students. There are many parts that request students to explore sensitive issues by answering purposeful questions. It would be to each student's benefit and advantage to have his or her own workbook, to ensure privacy and encourage ownership.

---

[1] Trainer defined in manual is teacher, parent, counselor, mentor

Kids Navigating Life - Level 3

The workbooks are written to be used in a variety of settings, including the classroom, counselor's office, or at home—either with parental assistance if the students are young or more independently if the students are older. We do encourage guidance in both cases. To what degree is dependent on the needs of the students and the environment in which the students are learning.

Workbooks

The Kids Navigating Life courseware is a set of four workbooks. The workbooks correlate with grade, age, and developmental milestones as identified in Table 1.

Developmental milestones, also referred to as developmental stages, are cumulative. The Kids Navigating Life courseware is developed accordingly. For example, a child knows how to identify the feelings of others because he first learned to identify his own. The courseware is developed in the same manner: building new skills on top of those skills the child has been exposed to or acquired at an earlier stage or in an earlier life skills workbook.

Table 1

Workbook	Grade	Age	Developmental Milestones
One	First	6	• Beginning to see others' point of view • Makes distinctions between members of the same racial or cultural group • Able to identify own feelings • Able to identify dangerous situations
One	Second	7	• Able to identify feelings of others • Shows listening skills • Acquires racial constancy • Shows appreciation and anger appropriately
One	Third	8	• Able to negotiate • Able to recognize mood changes • Able to understand feelings of shame and pride
Two	Fourth	9	• Better communication skills – uses listening skills • Able to resolve conflicts • Knows stressors
Two	Fifth	10	• Uses teamwork • Knows the strength of a diverse team • Increased decision-making and problem-solving skills • Begins to set personal goals
Two	Sixth	11	• Recognizes positive and negative friendships • Increased anger management skills • Knows appropriate ways to build relationships

Trainer's Manual

Workbook	Grade	Age	Developmental Milestones
Three	Seventh	12	• Able to communicate clearly • Able to pass on leadership where appropriate
Three	Eighth	13	• Can analyze consequences to actions • Developing advanced reasoning and abstract thinking skills • Establishing an identity, autonomy, and intimacy
Four	Ninth	14	• Can analyze how behaviors affect others • Can evaluate the effect of the media on self and groups
Four	Tenth	15	• Knows strategies for coping with feelings • Can acknowledge strengths of others • Is interested in personal achievement
Four	Eleventh	16	• Can analyze progression of behaviors which lead to violence • Reacts to ideas rather than people
Four	Twelfth	17	• Adjusts information delivery to accommodate the receiver • Works well with diverse groups of people

Note: A child's age and grade level only provides a clue to the developmental stage, it does not determine it. This is just the simplest way to partner the child with the courseware. The information presented does increase in complexity and focus as the student progresses through the courses.

Course

The Kids Navigating Life workbooks each contain seven courses. Each course is an aspect of success and functioning such as *Communicating Effectively* and *Thinking Critically* along with the others listed within Table 2 below.

Table 2

	Workbook 1 (Grades 1-3)	Workbook 2 (Grades 4-6)	Workbook 3 (Grades 7-8)	Workbook 4 (Grades 9-12)
Course 1	Communicating Effectively	Communicating Effectively	Communicating Effectively	Communicating Effectively
Course 2	Dealing with Emotions	Dealing with Emotions	Dealing with Emotions	Dealing with Emotions
Course 3	Building Character	Building Character	Building Character	Building Character

Kids Navigating Life - Level 3

	Workbook 1 (Grades 1-3)	Workbook 2 (Grades 4-6)	Workbook 3 (Grades 7-8)	Workbook 4 (Grades 9-12)
Course 4	Thinking Critically	Thinking Critically	Thinking Critically	Thinking Critically
Course 5	Gaining Social Skills	Gaining Social Skills	Gaining Social Skills	Gaining Social Skills
Course 6	Planning a Project	Planning a Project	Planning a Project	Planning a Project
Course 7	Making a Difference	Making a Difference	Making a Difference	Making a Difference

There are multiple skills which support each course in Table 2. These skills are defined, discussed, explored, and practiced. Table 3 identifies the skills in each of the courses.

Table 3

Course	Skills
Course 1: Communicating Effectively	Listening, Speaking, Observation
Course 2: Dealing with Emotions	Fear, Worry, Anger, Frustration
Course 3: Building Character	Respect, Trust, Loyalty, Responsibility
Course 4: Thinking Critically	Problem Solving, Decision Making, Resolving and Managing Conflict, Negotiating, Researching
Course 5: Gaining Social Skills	Social Interaction, Table Manners, Personal Grooming, Proper Clothing, Basic Courtesies
Course 6: Planning a Project	Time Management, Organization, Prioritizing, Adaptability, Teamwork, Evaluation
Course 7: Making a Difference	Commitment, Leadership, Diversity, Support of Others, Service to Others

Trainer's Manual

Format

The format is the same for all workbooks and each course as shown in Table 4 and includes the following:

Table 4

Course Table of Contents	Summary
Learning Outcomes	A list of what the students will know and be able to do upon completion of the course.
Course Introduction	A summary of the skills, activities, and outcomes for the course.
New Words	Age appropriate definitions and examples of words used in the course and possibly new to students.
Define It	A quick review of the New Words constructed to promote recall of the new information.
Test Yourself (Pretest)	Assesses the knowledge base of students before they begin the course. It is also the first opportunity for students to recall and further solidify the material they have been exposed to.
Course Scenario	Scenario and questions exposing students to the skills they will later practice.
What About You?	Introspective work that relates to an aspect of the Course Scenario.
Scenario Activity Practice	Activities relating to the scenario that encourage students to practice the skills they have been exposed to.
Show Your Skills	Activities used to encourage students to practice the skills they have been exposed to.
What About You?	Introspective activity that relates to the specific topic.
Test Yourself (Posttest)	Assesses the knowledge base of students after they have completed the course.
Congratulations	Recaps skills the student learned or practiced and a self-assessment of what skills students think they are good at and need more practice.

Kids Navigating Life - Level 3

In Workbook One and Workbook Two, an adult will need to provide assistance with reading and directions. In Workbook Three and Workbook Four, they should be able to navigate through most of their workbook with minimal assistance.

Many activities, in all levels, ask students to "pick a partner" or "find a group" in order to complete a task. Any of these exercises can be completed with just one other individual—another student, a teacher, a counselor, a parent, or a sibling.

Many of the exercises in the workbook will direct students to write down events, feelings, problems, or situations that could be private or emotionally charged. If a student becomes upset while working through these activities, it would be beneficial to stop for a while. It is not the intent of any exercise to overwhelm, upset, or create anxiety. The goal is to explore issues and expand understanding in order to build successful skills for navigating life.

Let's navigate through a workbook together.

Immediately after the workbook title there is a list of skills that directly relate to that course. These skills are the foundation for navigating life and are essential for success at any age.

In Workbook One and Workbook Two, these skills are defined using kid-friendly language and discussed in a very easy manner. This is the initial exposure to the material.

In Workbook Three, these skills are defined using increased vocabulary terms and presented in a more challenging way. This is where students have the opportunity to practice the skills they've learned and participate in discussion with others.

In Workbook Four, the skills are minimally defined, assuming prior knowledge of concepts, but offered up for mastery through intense discussion, personal exploration, participation in activities, and understanding others' perspectives.

The **Learning Outcomes** details what students will know and be able to do upon completion of that course. This is a quick outline for teachers, counselors, and/or parents to use as a guide when matching a child with the appropriate course level. If the objectives sound too advanced for a student, it may be more effective to begin with a lower course level.

In Workbook One and Workbook Two, the outcomes are compatible with initial exposure to the material.

In Workbook Three, the outcomes are compatible with the opportunity to practice skills and participate in discussion.

In Workbook Four, the outcomes are compatible with additional practice and mastery of the information.

The **Course Introduction** is a summary of what is included. It outlines the skills students will become familiar with, the activities requested of them, and a brief outcome of completion.

Trainer's Manual

The **New Words** section is where the skills are defined, as well as any terms frequently used in the course that would most likely be new to students. Words are defined using age-appropriate definitions and examples.

Define It is set up as a quick review of the New Words. It is constructed in question and answer format to promote recall of the new information. Subtle differences can be seen between workbooks in order to meet the students where they are educationally.

Test Yourself is students' first opportunity to recall the new information on paper and further solidify the material they will be exposed to throughout the course. This pretest is also a tool the trainer will use to determine students' knowledge of the skill before beginning the course.

In Workbook One and Workbook Two, the Test Yourself section is a bit silly as well as a bit serious. Again, the goal, through repetition, is to promote recall of the new information. The funny format provides a lighthearted break in the midst of sometimes difficult material and helps to break down defenses by promoting accomplishment.

In Workbook Three and Workbook Four, the format changes to a more age-appropriate tone while continuing with the goal of recall through repetition.

The **Course Scenario** is where students read about and relate to situations that others are in and have the opportunity to explore whether these kinds of things have ever happened to them. This section also provides investigatory opportunities that directly relate to the specific skills and exposes students to the skills they will later practice.

In all levels, the Course Scenario employs age-appropriate situations and encourages students to use reading comprehension skills to answer questions and reasoning to provide information that would assist the individuals in the scenario.

The **What About You** portion of the course is geared toward having students do some introspective work that relates to an aspect of the Course Scenario.

Students using Workbook One and Workbook Two are posed several questions that include identifying who they could turn to when help is needed and encouraging them to ask for help from others.

Students using Workbook Three and Workbook Four have the same types of questions, as well as more in-depth discovery of how they have been affected by situations similar to the one in the Course Scenario.

Scenario Activity Practice uses activities, exercises, and questions to encourage students to practice the skills they have been exposed to. There are examples to promote self-paced learning, group activities to bolster student involvement, and individual assignments to foster reflective thinking.

Show Your Skills utilizes the knowledge students have gained about the skills in order to complete the actions requested.

Kids Navigating Life - Level 3

In Workbook One and Workbook Two, the activities are compatible with initial exposure to the material.

In Workbook Three, the activities are compatible with the opportunity to practice skills and participate in discussion.

In Workbook Four, the activities are compatible with additional practice and mastery of the information.

The second **What About You** is again geared toward having students participate in an introspective exercise that relates to the specific topic.

Test Yourself is a written post test for the materials presented and acts as a barometer of students' comprehension. This can be used as a guide for rate of progression through the course. Each post test is a duplicate of the pretest found in the beginning of the course.

The **Congratulations! You Did It** section is the final portion of each course. It begins with a recap of some of the skills students learned or practiced and offers a self-assessment of where students feel they need further practice. Students are encouraged to identify a person to whom they can go for help and a positive assessment tool where they can note the skills they feel accomplished in.

Each course includes all of the sections above, in varying levels of difficulty that correspond to age and grade. Workbook One (grades 1-3) will contain the same information as Workbook Four (grades 9-12), but the delivery of the information is different.

Note: The activities and exercises are created to match developmental milestones for each grade level. For example, a high school student's developmental milestones include an emerging understanding that his or her actions can have far-reaching consequences; whereas an elementary school student does not typically have that high of a level of conscious awareness of how his or her actions impact others. The activities and exercises do not exceed the average level of development.

Kids Navigating Life workbooks have been created and developed to be an invaluable tool to assist parents, teachers, counselors, and others in an effort to help our youth develop solid internal compasses in order that they may be better equipped to navigate life, its challenges, and its opportunities.

In addition, we suggest you use our skills book, *Living Well, Working Smart: Soft Skills for Success*, as a teaching aid for step-by-step instructions on how to acquire and become proficient in the use of any one of the 41 skills listed.

For more information and to place an order:

The Mackey Group, LLC
P.O. Box 1247
Issaquah, WA 98027-1247
Phone: 425-391-8776
www.mackeygroup.com
info@mackeygroup.com

Course 1

Communicating Effectively

Skills
Listening

Speaking

Observing

Learning Outcomes:

Upon completing this course the student will be able to:

1. Express thoughts in a manner that is easily understood

2. Focus on a speaker and listen without interrupting

3. Organize thoughts to communicate effectively while under stress

Course Introduction:

The student will become familiar with terms used in the skill areas of effective speaking, listening, and observation. They will also be exposed to the skills necessary to communicate effectively under stress.

Communication skills will be practiced and feelings attributing to stress will be identified and discussed.

Kids Navigating Life - Level 3

 **NEW WORDS!**

Listening: Listening is such an important skill; you listen to sounds every day—your dog barks, your mom talks on the phone, your best friend tells you about a new kid in school. Being a good listener means you focus your attention on what someone is saying and don't speak until the person is done.

Speaking: Effective speaking is a skill that is very important at school and at home. It means you organize your thoughts and put them into words that people can understand. If they don't understand, you reorganize your thoughts to figure out a way to say it again. The goal is to be understood. The consequences to not organizing your thoughts before speaking are miscommunication and conflict.

Observation: Observation means to watch. You can learn a lot of things by watching. This is another skill that people use every day. For example, when you're listening, what do you do to make sure the speaker knows you are a good listener? You give really good eye contact, nod your head, make facial expressions, and show the speaker respect by waiting until he or she is finished before you talk.

Communicating Effectively

 **DEFINE IT!**

What does it mean to **focus** on a speaker?
> To **focus** on a speaker means to listen to what the person is saying and don't speak until the person is done.

What does it mean to **interrupt** someone?
> To **interrupt** means to talk while the person is already talking.

What does it mean to be a **good listener**?
> To be a **good listener** means to pay attention.

What is a **consequence**?
> A **consequence** is a good or bad result of actions and/or inactions.

What does it mean to be an **effective speaker**?
> **Effective speaking** means you organize your thoughts and put them into words that people can understand.

What does it mean to show **respect** to the speaker?
> To show respect means to listen without interrupting and make good eye contact.

What does it mean **to be understood**?
> **To be understood** means someone knew what you meant by what you said.

Kids Navigating Life - Level 3

TEST YOURSELF!

Pretest: Circle the correct answers and fill in the blanks to the questions.

1. What does it mean to **focus** on a speaker?
    A. Directed attention
    B. A point of concentration
    C. All of the above

2. What does it mean to **interrupt** someone?
    A. To break in with questions or remarks when another is speaking
    B. To allow the speaker to finish speaking before you begin to speak
    C. All of the above

3. What does it mean to be a **good listener**?
    A. To interrupt when someone is speaking
    B. To hear something with thoughtful attention
    C. All of the above

4. What is a **consequence**?
    A. A good or bad result of actions or inactions
    B. Something produced by a cause
    C. All of the above

5. What does it mean to be an **effective speaker**?
    A. To organize your thoughts and put them into words that people can understand
    B. To yell before a group
    C. All of the above

Communicating Effectively

6. What does it mean to show **respect** to the speaker?
    A. To listen without interrupting and make good eye contact
    B. An act of giving particular attention
    C. All of the above

7. What does it mean **to be understood**?
    A. Someone knew what you meant by what you said
    B. To grasp the meaning of
    C. All of the above

8. What does it mean to affect someone by something you say?
    A. Someone has a feeling or reaction
    B. Someone makes a decision that is influenced by your words
    C. All of the above

Advanced Question:

How can body language, movements and gestures, change the meaning of something you say?

_____

_____

_____

Kids Navigating Life - Level 3

COURSE SCENARIO

In each course of the workbook, you will read about a pretend situation, or scenario. These situations will give you a chance to apply the skills of the course as you are learning about them. As you read the scenario, think about your own life and if this has ever happened to you, then answer the questions at the end.

During class, Jessica thought Emily whispered that she liked Jonathon. Jessica had already told Emily that she liked Jonathon. She was mad at Emily for saying she liked him too. Jessica decided she was not going to speak to Emily for the rest of the day. After class, Emily walked up to Jessica and started telling her how much she liked Jonathon's cool skater backpack. The look on Jessica's face showed she was confused. She thought Emily had whispered she liked Jonathon and it was his backpack she liked.

MAKING IT REAL:

1. Has this ever happened to you? Yes ❑ No ❑

2. What did you do? _____
   _____

3. Why was Jessica **confused**? _____
   _____

4. What did Emily say that was not heard by Jessica? _____
   _____

5. What was the **consequence** of the miscommunication? _____
   _____

6. How could Jessica and Emily do this differently so there isn't miscommunication?
   _____
   _____

Communicating Effectively

WHAT ABOUT YOU?

1. Do you speak so others understand?
   Yes ☐ No ☐

2. Do you listen with the intent to understand?
   Yes ☐ No ☐

3. Do you organize your thoughts before you speak?
   Yes ☐ No ☐

4. If the listener doesn't understand, do you reorganize your thoughts and try again so the listener does understand?
   Yes ☐ No ☐

5. Identify a negative consequence of being misunderstood when you speak.
   _____

6. Identify a negative consequence of misunderstanding what has been said.
   _____

7. Do you ever feel frustrated when you're trying to communicate and others don't understand you? _____ Yes ☐ No ☐
   If yes, why? _____
   _____

8. Who can you go to for help or support when you feel frustrated?
   _____
   _____

Kids Navigating Life - Level 3

SCENARIO ACTIVITY PRACTICE!

The Whispering Game

Number of people: Three or more

The first person whispers one of the sentences below into the next person's ear. Then that person whispers what they THINK they heard into the next person's ear. Then that person whispers what they think they heard into the next person's ear. This continues until everyone has had a chance to hear and whisper the sentence. When done, the last person speaks the sentence out loud for everyone to hear.

1. Gertie's great-grandma grew aghast at Gertie's grammar.
2. Fat frogs flying past fast.
3. Six sharp smart sharks.
4. Betty and Bob brought back blue balloons from the big bazaar.
5. Listen to the local yokel yodel.
6. Kris Kringle carefully crunched on candy canes.
7. Two toads, totally tired.
8. Cows graze in groves on grass which grows in grooves in groves.
9. Selfish shellfish.

Play the game two times and then answer the questions below.

1. Write down the first sentence chosen: _____

   _____

2. What was the sentence that the last person said? _____

   _____

3. Was it different than what was originally whispered? Yes ❏ No ❏

Communicating Effectively

Why do you think this happens? _____
_____

4. Write down the second sentence chosen. _____
_____

5. What was the sentence that the last person said? _____
_____

6. Was it different than what was originally whispered? Yes ☐ No ☐

7. Do you think people were listening with the intent of understanding?
    Yes ☐ No ☐

8. Do you think people were speaking or whispering with the intent of being understood?
    Yes ☐ No ☐

Kids Navigating Life - Level 3

SHOW YOUR SKILLS!

Pick a partner.

Tell your partner what your favorite food is and why it's your favorite food.

Your partner is going to show you he or she understands what you are saying by telling you what your favorite food is and why it's your favorite food, using his or her own words.

Switch roles and do it again.

Tell your partner what your favorite TV show is and why it's your favorite TV show.

Your partner is going to show you he or she understands what you are saying by telling you what your favorite TV show is and why it's your favorite TV show, using his or her own words.

Communicating Effectively

WHAT ABOUT YOU?

Speaker:

Was there miscommunication?   Yes ❑   No ❑

Was it due to what you said or how you said it?   Yes ❑   No ❑

What could you do differently? _____

_____

_____

Listener:

Was there miscommunication?   Yes ❑   No ❑

Was there miscommunication due to what you thought you heard?
   Yes ❑   No ❑

What could you do differently? _____

_____

_____

Kids Navigating Life - Level 3

TEST YOURSELF!

Post Test: Circle the correct answers and fill in the blanks to the questions.

1. What does it mean to **focus** on a speaker?
    A. Directed attention
    B. A point of concentration
    C. All of the above

2. What does it mean to **interrupt** someone?
    A. To break in with questions or remarks when another is speaking
    B. To allow the speaker to finish speaking before you begin to speak
    C. All of the above

3. What does it mean to be a **good listener**?
    A. To interrupt when someone is speaking
    B. To hear something with thoughtful attention
    C. All of the above

4. What is a **consequence**?
    A. A good or bad result of actions or inactions
    B. Something produced by a cause
    C. All of the above

5. What does it mean to be an **effective speaker**?
    A. To organize your thoughts and put them into words that people can understand
    B. To yell before a group
    C. All of the above

Communicating Effectively

6. What does it mean to show **respect** to the speaker?
    A. To listen without interrupting and make good eye contact
    B. An act of giving particular attention
    C. All of the above

7. What does it mean **to be understood**?
    A. Someone knew what you meant by what you said
    B. To grasp the meaning of
    C. All of the above

8. What does it mean to affect someone by something you say?
    A. Someone has a feeling or reaction
    B. Someone makes a decision that is influenced by your words
    C. All of the above

Advanced Question:

How can body language, movements and gestures, change the meaning of something you say?

_____

_____

_____

_____

Kids Navigating Life - Level 3

CONGRATULATIONS! YOU DID IT!

You did it! You have just learned some of the skills you need to communicate effectively! Great job! You helped Jessica and Emily with their problem, and you figured out people who you could go to if you are frustrated. You practiced being a good listener and good speaker. And, you practiced making observations.

For extra credit answer these questions:

Which skills do I still need to practice?
- ❑ Speaking
- ❑ Listening
- ❑ Observation
- ❑ Focusing

Who can I ask to help me practice these skills?

_____

_____

Which skills am I really good at?
- ❑ Speaking
- ❑ Listening
- ❑ Observation
- ❑ Focusing

Keep going! There is so much to learn that will help make your life better!

You are doing great!

Course 2

Dealing with Emotions

Skills
Fear
Worry
Anger
Embarrassment

Learning Outcomes

Upon completing this course the student will be able to:

1. Use fear to their benefit

2. Move out of fear and into being proactive

3. Move out of worry and into being proactive

4. Turn anger into a motivator for change

5. Move out of being embarrassed to being confident

Course Introduction

The student will become familiar with terms used in the skill areas of managing fear, worry, anger, and embarrassment. They will also identify how these emotions feel to them. Identifying difficult emotions will be practiced.

Kids Navigating Life - Level 3

 **NEW WORDS!**

Emotions: Emotions are feelings we all have. Emotions are felt in our minds and our bodies. For example, if you feel embarrassed, your hands might sweat, your face might feel hot, and you might have feelings of being nervous. This is because our bodies respond to emotions. You might smile when you are happy or cry when you are sad.

Fear: Fear means to feel afraid of something. Fear can be used as a beneficial emotion. Fear can also keep you safe. An example might be that you fear you will forget your locker combination. Using fear as a benefit to you might mean you turn that fear into action and memorize your locker combination or keep the combination in your folder.

Worry: Worry means to feel upset or to be concerned about something. An example is you might worry about being late to school. Using worry as a benefit to you might mean you turn that worry into action and set your alarm to wake you up five minutes early, you double check your alarm before you go to bed, and/or you get all of your stuff ready the night before.

Stress: Stress means to feel anxious or worry constantly. An example is you might feel stressed if you told a lie to your parents two weeks ago and you worry you will get caught. Using stress as a benefit to you might mean that your stress causes you to admit the truth and apologize for lying.

Anger: Anger means to feel really mad or very annoyed. An example is you might feel anger if you get an F on a test. Using anger as a benefit to you might mean you turn that anger into energy, and you study harder for the tests so you don't get F's on your tests.

Embarrassed: Embarrassed means to feel uncomfortable, self-conscious, or humiliated. An example is you might feel embarrassed if you are picked last for a team. Using being embarrassed as a benefit to you might mean you turn that feeling of embarrassment into the challenge of becoming better at that sport.

Mood: A mood is the way you choose to behave, or your frame of mind. We can always learn something from the mood we are in. It may be a little bit of knowledge or a big piece. For example, you are in a bad mood because you woke up late, and you choose to be mean to your best friend. What can you learn from this? Is it your best friend's fault you woke up late? No, you are mad at yourself for being late. Your mood is your responsibility. Also to note, if you choose to continue to treat your friends poorly because you are in a bad mood, you may lose your friends.

Dealing with Emotions

 **DEFINE IT!**

What are **emotions**?

Emotions are feelings we all have. Emotions are felt in our minds and our bodies.

What does **fear** mean?

Fear means to feel afraid of something. Fear can be used as a beneficial emotion. Fear can also keep you safe.

What does **worry** mean?

Worry means to feel upset or to be concerned about something.

What does **stress** mean?

Stress means to feel anxious or worry constantly.

What does **anger** mean?

Anger means to feel really mad or very annoyed.

What does **embarrassed** mean?

Embarrassed means to feel uncomfortable, self-conscious, or humiliated.

What does **mood** mean?

A **mood** means the way you choose to behave, or your frame of mind.

Kids Navigating Life - Level 3

TEST YOURSELF!

Pretest: Circle the correct answers.

1. What are **emotions**?
    - A. Feelings we all have
    - B. Feelings no one has
    - C. All the above

2. What does **fear** mean?
    - A. To feel afraid of something
    - B. A be afraid of nothing
    - C. All the above

3. What does **worry** mean?
    - A. To be happy
    - B. To be concerned about something
    - C. All the above

4. What does **stress** mean?
    - A. To feel anxious
    - B. To relax
    - C. All the above

5. What does **anger** mean?
    - A. To feel really mad
    - B. To laugh
    - C. All the above

Dealing with Emotions

6. What does **embarrassed** mean?
    A. To feel uncomfortable
    B. To feel self-conscious
    C. To feel calm
    D. All the above

7. What does **mood** mean?
    A. The way you choose to behave
    B. Frame of mind
    C. Your willpower
    D. All the above

Kids Navigating Life - Level 3

COURSE SCENARIO!

In each course of this workbook is a pretend situation, or a scenario. Read the story and answer the questions. Think about if this has ever happened to you.

It's Friday afternoon, and Julie has tried out for the school volleyball team. The cuts are happening on Monday. She will know then if she has made the team or if she has been cut. Julie is worried about if she's made the team or not and afraid that her best friend, who has also tried out for the team, will make the team and she won't.

Monday morning comes and Julie learns that she didn't make the team. Her best friend did. Julie is embarrassed and wants to go home. All day long people are asking her if she made the team, and she has to tell them, "No." By the end of the day, Julie is angry that she didn't make it and thinks the coaches are all wrong. She is also angry at her best friend for making the team, and she feels left behind.

MAKING IT REAL

1. Have you ever felt left out? Yes ❑ No ❑

2. What was the situation? _____
   _____
   _____

3. List the **emotions** that Julie had in the above scenario. _____
   _____
   _____

4. Why was Julie **worried**? _____
   _____

Dealing with Emotions

5. Why was Julie **afraid**? _____

    _____

6. Why was Julie **embarrassed**? _____

    _____

7. Why was Julie **angry**? _____

    _____

8. If Julie chooses to stay **angry** at her friend for making the team, could she lose her friend? Yes ❑ No ❑ Why?

    _____

    _____

9. This is obviously very hard for Julie, but how can she support her friend?

    _____

    _____

Kids Navigating Life - Level 3

WHAT ABOUT YOU?

1. What do you **worry** about? _____
   _____
   _____

2. How can you use **worry** to your benefit? _____
   _____
   _____

3. What are your **fears**? _____
   _____
   _____

4. How can you use **fear** to your benefit? _____
   _____
   _____

5. When do you get **embarrassed**? _____
   _____
   _____

6. How can you turn being **embarrassed** into a challenge? _____
   _____
   _____

Dealing with Emotions

7. What do you get **angry** about? _____
   _____
   _____

8. How can you use **anger** to your benefit? _____
   _____
   _____

9. Who can you talk to about feeling **anger**? _____
   _____
   _____

10. Who can you talk to about what you **worry** about? _____
    _____
    _____

11. Who can you talk to about feeling **embarrassed**? _____
    _____
    _____

12. Who can you talk to about feeling **fear**? _____
    _____
    _____

Kids Navigating Life - Level 3

SCENARIO ACTIVITY PRACTICE!

Tip of the Iceberg

In this activity you will identify the underlying reasons for feeling anger, fear, worry, or embarrassment.

Let's look at emotions as an iceberg. When you see an iceberg in the ocean, you are only seeing the very tip. What you don't see underneath the water is the base of the iceberg which is mammoth in size.

In this example, the tip of the iceberg is the emotion. Underneath the water are the reasons for the emotion or the issue.

Example: Julie is angry. She didn't make the volleyball team. **Anger** is what we see on the tip of the iceberg which is the emotion. The reasons Julie is angry are at the base of the iceberg underneath the water.

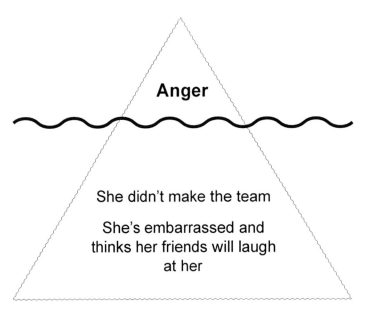

In order for Julie to identify and understand why she is feeling angry, she needs to answer these questions.

Julie writes:

1. I am feeling _angry_ about _the fact that I didn't make the team_.
          Emotion   **Issue**

24

Dealing with Emotions

2. Why am I feeling __angry__ about __the fact that I didn't make the team__?
                         Emotion   **Issue**

   Because I was embarrassed that people knew I tried out for the team, and now I'm not on the team. They know I didn't make it.

Question to Julie: Is this issue yours, the coaches, or your friend's?

3. Is there anything I can do to change the situation? Yes ☐ No ☐ Maybe ☒
   What can I do?

   I can ask for another chance to try out for the team

4. What can I do to turn the emotion into something that can benefit me or someone else? *I can direct my anger into becoming better at volleyball by practicing harder for next year's tryouts. I can play a different sport. I can get involved in another activity. I can be a good friend and support my friend at the games.*

5. What is the worst thing that could happen? *My friends will make fun of me because I didn't make the team.*

6. Can I deal with the worst thing that could happen? Yes ☒ No ☐

   If no, who can I talk to about this or go to for help? _____

7. Instead of getting __angry__, what can I do differently next time something like this happens?   **Emotion**

   I can try to identify the real reason why I'm feeling angry and/or who I'm really angry with and deal with that instead of blaming others.

8. Do I need to ask for help? Yes ☒ No ☐ If yes, who can I ask for help?

   I can ask the coach, my parents, or a teacher for help.

Kids Navigating Life - Level 3

SHOW YOUR SKILLS!

Tip of the Iceberg

Write down the emotion you are having in the tip of the iceberg.

Write down the reasons you are feeling the emotion in the base of the iceberg.

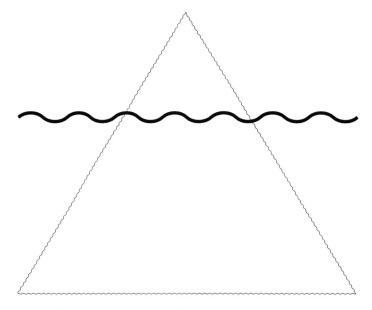

In order for you to identify and understand why you are having the emotion you are having, answer these questions.

1. I am feeling _____ about _____ .
                   Emotion   **Issue**

2. Why am I feeling _____ about _____ ?
                   Emotion   **Issue**

_____

Question: Whose issue is this? Mine _____ Someone else's _____

Dealing with Emotions

3. Is there anything I can do to change the situation? Yes ☐ No ☐ Maybe ☐

   What can I do? _____

   _____

   _____

4. What can I do to turn the emotion into something that can benefit me or someone else? _____

   _____

   _____

5. What is the worst thing that could happen? _____

   _____

   _____

6. Can I deal with the worst thing that could happen? Yes ☐ No ☐

   If no, who can I talk to about this or go to for help? _____

7. Instead of getting _____, what can I do differently next time something like this happens?　　　**Emotion**

   _____

   _____

8. Do I need to ask for help? Yes ☐ No ☐ If yes, who can I ask for help?

   _____

Kids Navigating Life - Level 3

WHAT ABOUT YOU?

1. Do you **worry** about things you have no control over? Yes ❑ No ❑

   If so, what are the things you worry about?

   _____
   _____

2. Do you have **fears** that stop you from doing what you want to do? Yes ❑ No ❑

   If so, what are they?

   _____
   _____

3. Do you let the **fear** of embarrassing yourself stop you from doing what you are interested in doing? Yes ❑ No ❑

   If so, what can you do to change that fear and use it to motivate you?

   _____
   _____

4. Do you get **angry** over what you can't control? Yes ❑ No ❑

   If yes, what can you do to change that anger and use it to motivate you?

   _____
   _____

Dealing with Emotions

5. Do you get **angry** and blame others when things don't go your way?

    Yes ❏ No ❏

    If yes, what can you do to identify what the real reason is behind feeling **angry**?

    _____
    _____

6. What **mood** are you in right now? Angry, embarrassed, worried, fearful?

    _____

    Why?

    _____
    _____

7. What can you do to change your **mood** right now?

    _____
    _____

Kids Navigating Life - Level 3

TEST YOURSELF!

Post Test: Circle the correct answers.

1. What are **emotions**?
    - A. Feelings we all have
    - B. Feelings no one has
    - C. All the above

2. What does **fear** mean?
    - A. To feel afraid of something
    - B. A be afraid of nothing
    - C. All the above

3. What does **worry** mean?
    - A. To be happy
    - B. To be concerned about something
    - C. All the above

4. What does **stress** mean?
    - A. To feel anxious
    - B. To relax
    - C. All the above

5. What does **anger** mean?
    - A. To feel really mad
    - B. To laugh
    - C. All the above

Dealing with Emotions

6. What does **embarrassed** mean?
    - A. To feel uncomfortable
    - B. To feel self-conscious
    - C. To feel calm
    - D. All the above

7. What does **mood** mean?
    - A. The way you choose to behave
    - B. Frame of mind
    - C. Your willpower
    - D. All the above

Kids Navigating Life - Level 3

CONGRATULATIONS!

YOU DID IT! You have just learned how to identify some difficult emotions we all have. Great job! You identified Julie's feelings about not making the volleyball team. Then you looked at how to turn difficult emotions into actions that could benefit you or someone else. You also identified what emotions you have and the reasons why you have them.

For extra credit answer these questions:

Which emotions do I still need to learn more about?
- ❏ Fear
- ❏ Worry
- ❏ Anger
- ❏ Embarrassed

Who can I ask to help me practice these skills?

_____

_____

Which emotions do I understand?
- ❏ Fear
- ❏ Worry
- ❏ Anger
- ❏ Embarrassed

Keep going! There is so much to learn that will help make your life better!

You are doing great!

Course 3

Building Character

<u>Skills</u>
Respect
Trust
Loyalty
Responsibility

Learning Outcomes

Upon completing this course the student will be able to:

1. Identify character traits of self and others

2. Describe a loyal and trusting friend

3. Identify what it means to be respectful of others

4. Describe what it means to take responsibility

5. Define ethics and morals

Course Introduction

The student will become familiar with terms used in the skill areas of respect, loyalty, trust, and responsibility. They will also identify how these skills manifest in their own life.

Character building skills will be practiced and emotions associated with lack of knowledge, and inappropriate behavior of self and others will be identified and discussed.

Kids Navigating Life - Level 3

 **NEW WORDS!**

Character: We each have character. Our character is made up of qualities or traits that make us different from one another. We can choose if we want to be someone with good character or bad character.

Character traits: Character traits are the qualities that make up your character. They can be good or bad. Some examples of character traits are being brave, kind, rude, lazy, and loyal.

Respect: To respect means to be nice and polite to people. It also means to look to them for wisdom, guidance, direction, or advice. People that you may respect are your parents, your teachers, a relative, or family friend.

Trust: To trust means to rely on the character, truth, or strength of someone or something. For example, you may trust your dad or mom to always be there for you when you have a problem. You may trust yourself to do the right thing.

Loyalty: To show loyalty means to be faithful to someone or something. For example, to show loyalty to your friend might mean helping them with their homework instead of going to the baseball game. To show loyalty to your school might mean wearing your school's colors on game day.

Responsibility: Responsibility means to be responsible. It means you are able to understand and answer for your actions whether right or wrong. For example, you understand that lying for your friend can get you into trouble, and when you are caught, you will answer for your actions. In other words, you will pay the consequence of lying for your friend.

Building Character

 **DEFINE IT!**

What is **character**?
   Character is the mixture of qualities that separate one person from another.

What are **character traits**?
   Character traits are the qualities you have. They can be positive or negative such as being brave, kind, rude, lazy, forgetful, calm, bossy, loyal, trustworthy, responsible, and respectful.

What does **respect** mean?
   To **respect** someone means to be nice and polite toward them. It also means to look to them for wisdom, guidance, direction, or advice.

What does **trust** mean?
   Trust means to rely on the character, truth, or strength of someone or something.

What is **loyalty**?
   To show **loyalty** means to be faithful to someone or something.

What does **responsibility** mean?
   Responsibility means to be responsible. It means you are able to understand and answer for your actions whether right or wrong.

What are **ethics**?
   Ethics are rules, standards, or principles of how one should behave in given situations. It is a code of conduct a person lives by.

What are **morals**?
   Morals are the concepts of what you think are good or bad. It is the way you judge someone in relation to your own concepts of what you think are good and bad.

Kids Navigating Life - Level 3

TEST YOURSELF!

Pretest: Circle the correct answers.

1. What is **character**?
    - A. A mixture of personal qualities
    - B. An actor in a play
    - C. All the above

2. What are **character traits**?
    - A. Positive or negative qualities
    - B. A style of painting
    - C. All of the above

3. What does **respect** mean?
    - A. To look to someone for wisdom, guidance, direction, or advice
    - B. To yell at your mom or dad after school
    - C. All the above

4. What does **trust** mean?
    - A. To rely on the character, truth, or strength of someone
    - B. To not rely on self
    - C. All the above

5. What does it mean to show **loyalty**?
    - A. To be faithful to someone
    - B. To be faithful to something such as a belief
    - C. All the above

6. What does **responsibility** mean?
    - A. To be responsible and accept consequences for your actions
    - B. To do everything not to be held accountable
    - C. All the above

Building Character

7. What are **ethics**?
    A. Rules or principles of how one should behave in given situations
    B. A code of conduct
    C. All the above

8. What are **morals**?
    A. The concepts of what you think are right and good
    B. A computer game character
    C. All of the above

Kids Navigating Life - Level 3

COURSE SCENARIO!

In each course of the workbook, you will read about a pretend situation, or scenario. These situations will give you a chance to apply the skills of the course as you are learning about them. As you read the scenario, think about your own life and if this has ever happened to you, then answer the questions at the end.

It's the day before school starts and Celeste decides to get her hair colored darker. Her family tells her it looks good. She's still a bit unsure but ready to start the new year. The first day back to school Celeste gets on the school bus and sits down. Her two best friends get on and walk right past her without saying hello. She looks back at them and says hello. They whisper, laugh, and tell her she looks "goth." Celeste was surprised her two best friends would make fun of her like that.

Right then and there Celeste made a decision. These were two people she could not trust to be loyal friends.

MAKING IT REAL

1. Has someone you considered a friend made fun of you in front of others?
    Yes ❑ No ❑

2. If yes, what did you do?

    _____
    _____

3. Was Celeste's **trust** of her friends hurt by their actions? Yes ❑ No ❑

4. Why do you think Celeste's friends would do this?

    _____
    _____

5. Would you consider Celeste's friends to be **loyal**? Yes ❑ No ❑
    Why or why not? _____
    _____

Building Character

6. If Celeste let herself be affected by what her friends said, how would she feel?

   _____

   _____

7. How would those feelings affect her day? _____

   _____

   _____

8. What **character traits** does Celeste have? _____

   _____

   _____

9. What **traits** are Celeste's friends demonstrating? _____

   _____

   _____

10. If you were Celeste's friend and overheard this, what would you do or say?

    _____

    _____

Kids Navigating Life - Level 3

WHAT ABOUT YOU?

1. What **character traits** do you have?

   _____
   _____

2. What **character traits** would you like to have that you don't think you have now?

   _____

3. What have you done to build **trust** with your friends?

   _____
   _____

4. What have you done to build **trust** with your parents?

   _____
   _____

5. Do you take **responsibility** for your actions or reactions? Yes ❑ No ❑

6. What are two things you have done that you have taken **responsibility** for?

   _____
   _____

7. Define what a **loyal** and **trusted** friend is to you.

   _____
   _____

Building Character

8. How do you show you **respect** yourself?

_____

_____

Kids Navigating Life - Level 3

SCENARIO ACTIVITY PRACTICE!

Build a Character Workshop

Here's your fantastic, fun opportunity to Build a Character! There is a big list of character traits for you to choose from. For each person listed, fill in four character traits that you think they had or have. Remember, character traits can be good or bad.

List of Character Traits

Brave	Neat	Outspoken	Rude	Dreamy	Fussy
Witty	Serious	Generous	Clever	Bossy	Stern
Reasonable	Kind	Patient	Fearful	Wise	Stubborn
Relaxed	Demanding	Cautious	Gentle	Obedient	Selfish
Fierce	Calm	Lazy	Loud	Polite	Sensitive
Tough	Playful	Awkward	Trusting	Shy	Forgetful
Honest	Cooperative	Forgiving	Sneaky	Timid	Loyal
Daring	Confused	Withdrawn	Sentimental	Organized	Gloomy
Suspicious	Intelligent	Ambitious	Helpful	Careless	Unkind
Boastful	Stingy	Mischievous	Greedy	Friendly	Charming
Courageous	Unfriendly	Understanding	Cruel	Pleasant	Curious
Self-centered	Dependable	Determined	Reckless	Talkative	Quiet

A President

_____
_____
_____
_____

Albert Einstein

_____
_____
_____
_____

Abe Lincoln

_____
_____
_____
_____

Your Favorite Actor

_____
_____
_____
_____

Your Favorite Athlete

_____
_____
_____
_____

Your Favorite Singer

_____
_____
_____
_____

Your Mom or Dad

_____
_____
_____
_____

Your Teacher or Coach

_____
_____
_____
_____

A Friend

_____
_____
_____
_____

Building Character

SHOW YOUR SKILLS!

The Character Scramble

Here are a bunch of character traits that are all scrambled. Your job is to un-scramble them using the List of Character Traits! Example: DUER This is actually the character trait RUDE.

List of CHARACTER TRAITS

Brave	Greedy	Shy	Honest
Witty	Selfish	Polite	Respectful
Neat	Responsible	Loyal	Tough
Demanding	Calm	Trusting	Helpful

EVRAB: _____

MCLA: _____

HSY: _____

EANT: _____

HNOTES: _____

LUFPLEH: _____

OLPTEI: _____

SSILFEH: _____

GHTUO: _____

YWTTI: _____

DNMEINGDA: _____

EEDRYG: _____

43

Kids Navigating Life - Level 3

Some really tough ones:

YOALL: _____

IRUTSTGN: _____

UPSREFETCL: _____

LSOERENIBPS: _____

What are the positive or negative qualities called that we all have but yet make us each different?

RRACCAHET   ISTTRA: _____

Nice work!

Building Character

WHAT ABOUT YOU?

Identify ten good and bad character traits that you have.

1. _____
2. _____
3. _____
4. _____
5. _____
6. _____
7. _____
8. _____
9. _____
10. _____

Identify ten character traits that you want to have.

1. _____
2. _____
3. _____
4. _____
5. _____
6. _____
7. _____
8. _____
9. _____
10. _____

What are **character traits** you would like to change? _____
_____

What can you do to change those **character traits** you don't like? _____
_____

What can you do to get the **character traits** you want to have? _____
_____

Kids Navigating Life - Level 3

TEST YOURSELF

Post Test: Circle the correct answers.

1. What is **character**?
    - A. A mixture of personal qualities
    - B. An actor in a play
    - C. All the above

2. What are **character traits**?
    - A. Positive or negative qualities
    - B. A style of painting
    - C. All of the above

3. What does **respect** mean?
    - A. To look to someone for wisdom, guidance, direction, or advice
    - B. To yell at your mom or dad after school
    - C. All the above

4. What does **trust** mean?
    - A. To rely on the character, truth, or strength of someone
    - B. To not rely on self
    - C. All the above

5. What does it mean to show **loyalty**?
    - A. To be faithful to someone
    - B. To be faithful to something such as a belief
    - C. All the above

6. What does **responsibility** mean?
    - A. To be responsible and accept consequences for your actions
    - B. To do everything not to be held accountable
    - C. All the above

Building Character

7. What are **ethics**?
    A. Rules or principles of how one should behave in given situations
    B. A code of conduct
    C. All the above

8. What are **morals**?
    A. The concepts of what you think are right and good
    B. A virtual character
    C. All of the above

Kids Navigating Life - Level 3

CONGRATULATIONS!

YOU DID IT! You have just learned some character building skills you need to succeed. You identified character traits in others and yourself. You identified what a loyal friend looks like and what it takes to build trust. You also learned what it means to take responsibility for your actions and reactions.

For extra credit answer these questions:

Which skills do I still need to practice?
- ❑ Respect
- ❑ Trust
- ❑ Loyalty
- ❑ Responsibility
- ❑ Identifying my emotions

Who can I ask to help me practice these skills?

_____

_____

Which skills am I really good at?
- ❑ Respect
- ❑ Trust
- ❑ Loyalty
- ❑ Responsibility
- ❑ Identifying my emotions

Keep going! There is so much to learn that will help make your life better!

You are doing great!

Course 4

Thinking Critically

Skills
Problem-solving

Decision-making

Resolving and Managing Conflict

Negotiating

Researching

Learning Outcomes

Upon completing this course the student will be able to

1. Define solution

2. Define decision

3. Identify the steps to finding an effective solution

4. Identify the affect the problem has on self and others

5. Identify possible cause or causes of a problem

6. Recognize the outcome needing to be achieved

Course Introduction

The student will become familiar with terms used in the skill areas of problem solving, decision making, conflict resolution or management, negotiating, and researching. They will also identify resources available to them to help solve a problem such as their parents, relatives, teachers, and the library or Internet.

Conflict management and resolution skills will be practiced and emotions associated with this skill area will be identified and discussed.

Kids Navigating Life - Level 3

 **NEW WORDS!**

Problem Solving: We all have problems from time to time and it seems we all deal with them in a different way. Some people just ignore problems and hope they will go away. This really does not work, and usually the problem gets worse. Some people deal with problems right away and move on. That is a better choice. It is important to find out where the problem started: its origin.

Decision Making: You have probably already made decisions today. If you think about it, everybody makes decisions almost all the time. Some decisions are easy, and some are hard. Even if you do not do anything you still made a decision. Good decisions have good results, or positive consequences. Bad decisions have bad results, or negative consequences. What was the last decision you made?

Resolving or Managing Conflict: Do you know what the word *conflict* means? It's like when things are not going right, or there is disagreement about something. We all have conflict sometimes. Lots of times, you can manage or solve the conflict; sometimes you can't. When there is conflict, there are strong feelings to deal with, like anger or frustration. The quicker you deal with the conflict, the easier your life can be.

Negotiating: Negotiating is a skill that we use every day. *Thinking critically* plays a big role in the ability to apply this skill. To negotiate means to figure something out by talking with someone, so you get what you want, or what works for you, and they get what they want, or what works for them. It's like "making a deal" with someone. Let's say you are at home and you would like pizza for dinner. Your mom wants your room cleaned. You could negotiate a deal with her (it may or may not work, and that is sometimes what happens in negotiating): Maybe you clean your room, and she makes pizza for dinner. You talked with your mom to see what she wanted, and you told her what you wanted, you "made a deal." That is negotiating. When we negotiate, we use skills like problem solving, decision making, and conflict resolution to find an outcome that works for everyone involved.

Researching: When you need to solve a problem or a conflict or write a paper on a specific topic you sometimes need to do research to get more information. Researching is collecting bits and pieces of knowledge that will help you to make a final decision, understand the origin of a problem, or finish writing your term paper. You would not want to make an important decision without first knowing all the facts, and you would not try to write a paper on Zimbabwe without knowing anything about the place--you need to do research to be informed. It is an important skill to have.

Thinking Critically

DEFINE IT!

What is a **solution**?

A **solution** is: An answer to a problem

What does **outcome** mean?

The end result after an action.

Examples:

If I break my computer, I will not be able to use it.
(ACTION: I broke my computer. OUTCOME: I cannot use it.)

If I do not get good grades, I will not be able to play sports.
(ACTION: I did not get good grades. OUTCOME: I cannot play sports.)

If I resolve the conflict with my friend, we will be able to go to the movies together.
(ACTION: I resolve the conflict with my friend. OUTCOME: We go to the movies.)

What does **research** mean?
- The collecting of information
- The careful search for information

What are **needs** and **expectations**?

When you are working to solve a problem, make a decision, or resolve or manage conflict, it's important to figure out your **needs** and **expectations** and the **needs** and **expectations** of other people.

Needs: A need is something we require like air to breathe. It's more than a want. We all have needs. Whether or not we get our needs met is based on how we ask that they be met and who we ask.

Example: If you have a project that is due and you need your dad's help, how would you ask him so that he would want to help? Would you say, "Dad, I need you to help me NOW!" or would you say, "Dad, I have a project that is due in two days, and I need

Kids Navigating Life - Level 3

your help. It will take me about three hours to complete. Do you have some time today or tomorrow to help me?"

Expectations: An expectation is something you look for, look forward to, or wait for. We all have expectations.

Example: If it is your birthday and your mom has always baked you a cake, would you expect her to bake you a cake for this birthday? Most likely, yes. It's now expected because she's done it in the past. That makes it an expectation.

Thinking Critically

TEST YOURSELF

Pretest: Circle the correct answers and fill in the blanks to the questions.

1. What is a **solution**?
    A. An answer to a problem or an explanation
    B. Nose hair

2. What is an **outcome**?
    A. The end result after an action or inaction
    B. The sound a mad mouse would make

3. What does **decision making** mean?
    A. To work on making a decision based on all information
    B. To work on coming to a conclusion based on all information
    C. All of the above

4. What is an **origin**?
    A. Where something starts.
    B. The root of a problem or conflict.
    C. The source of the trouble.
    D. All of the above.

5. What do you need to find to solve a **problem**?
    A. The origin of the problem
    B. The origin of the conflict
    C. All of the above

6. How can you find an **origin** of a **problem** or **conflict**?
    A. Ask questions of others
    B. Talk about the problem with people involved
    C. Research books
    D. All of the above

Kids Navigating Life - Level 3

7. How do you determine what the **problem** is?
    A. Guess
    B. Gather information from people involved
    C. Talk to your pets
    D. All of the above

8. What is an **alternative solution**?
    A. A different solution than the one you came up with
    B. A different solution than the one you used
    C. All of the above

9. What does **win/win** mean?

    _____

    _____

    _____

10. What skill does it take to reach **win/win**?
    ☐ Conflict resolution or management
    ☐ Decision making
    ☐ Researching
    ☐ Negotiating
    ☐ Identifying my emotions

Advanced Question: How are conflict resolution and conflict management different from one another?

_____

_____

_____

Thinking Critically

COURSE SCENARIO!

In each course of the workbook, you will read about a situation. These situations will give you a chance to apply the skills of the course as you are learning about them. As you read the scenario, think about your own life and if this has ever happened to you, then answer the questions at the end.

Allison and Micah have been put in charge of working the snack bar at school. They can't stand one another. Allison used to make fun of Micah when they were in the fourth grade, and Micah used to always try to get Allison into trouble. Since then, they have always just ignored each another.

They start to work the snack bar and the cash register stops working. "Great!" yells Micah. Allison laughs at him and then realizes she won't be able to use the cash register either. She goes to find a teacher and can't. She tells Micah they are on their own. Allison knows how to fix things and Micah is very strong in math. How can they serve the students in line and manage the conflict between them? They start to talk about how they can solve the problem.

MAKING IT REAL

1. Has this ever happened to you? Yes ☐ No ☐

2. What did you do? _____
   _____

3. What **decisions** do Allison and Micah need to make? _____
   _____

4. What is the **outcome** they need to achieve? _____
   _____

5. What is a possible **solution**? _____
   _____

6. Is it important that Allison and Micah manage the **conflict** between them to get the job done? Yes ☐ No ☐

   Why? _____

Kids Navigating Life - Level 3

WHAT ABOUT YOU!

1. Talk about a **decision** you have had to make. _____

   _____

   _____

2. What information did you have to gather to make that **decision**? Where did you get the information?

   _____

   _____

   _____

3. Write down a **problem** you have had to solve.

   _____

   _____

4. What was a **solution** to that problem?

   _____

   _____

5. Did you have an **alternative solution** if your first solution did not work? If so, what was it?

   _____

   _____

   _____

Thinking Critically

SCENARIO ACTIVITY PRACTICE!

Statement, Impact, Cause, Outcome, Solutions

In the course scenario, Allison and Micah had two problems. The first problem was they had to work together when they did not like each other. The second problem was the cash register broke and needed to be fixed. These are the problems you must solve in this next activity.

The exercise is called **Statement, Impact, Cause, Outcome, and Solutions**. You need to do one of these for the first problem and one of these for the second problem. Imagine that you are in their position. Think about their situation as you read the questions and answer as best as you can.

First Problem: Allison and Micah have to work together even though they do not like each other.

1. Problem Statement: Gather accurate information from the scenario to determine what the problem is.	What is the **problem** you must solve?
2. Problem Impact: Consider how the problem will affect the people standing in line, how it will affect you individually, and how it will affect the school store if it loses money.	Who is affected by this **problem**? What are the benefits of solving this **problem**? What are the consequences if this **problem** is not solved?
3. Problem Cause: Try to figure out the cause of the problem. To do this, look closely at the issues with the people, process, and system involved.	What are the **causes** of this **problem**?
4. Outcome: Think about the outcome you want to achieve by solving this problem.	What is the **outcome** you want to achieve?

Kids Navigating Life - Level 3

5. Problem Solutions: Come up with possible solutions and possible alternative solutions. Note: A solution may require negotiation--a win/win for those involved.	What are some possible **solutions** to the problem? Solution 1: Solution 2: Solution 3: What are the possible positive and negative **effects** of each solution? Solution 1: Solution 2: Solution 3: Which of these **solutions** do you think will give you the **outcome** you want to achieve? Why?

Thinking Critically

SHOW YOUR SKILLS

Second Problem: The cash register is broken and needs to be fixed.

1. Problem Statement: Gather accurate information from the scenario to determine what the problem is.	What is the **problem** you must solve?
2. Problem Impact: Consider how the problem will affect the people standing in line, how it will affect you individually, and how it will affect the school store if it loses money.	Who is affected by this **problem**? What are the benefits of solving this **problem**? What are the consequences if this **problem** is not solved?
3. Problem Cause: Try to figure out the cause of the problem. To do this, look closely at the issues with the people, process, and system involved.	What are the **causes** of this **problem**?
4. Outcome: Think about the outcome you want to achieve by solving this problem.	What is the **outcome** you want to achieve?

Kids Navigating Life - Level 3

5. **Problem Solutions**: Come up with possible solutions and possible alternative solutions. Note: A solution may require negotiation—a win/win for those involved.	What are some possible **solutions** to the problem? Solution 1: Solution 2: Solution 3: What are the possible positive and negative **effects** of each solution? Solution 1: Solution 2: Solution 3: Which of these **solutions** do you think will give you the **outcome** you want to achieve? Why?

Thinking Critically

WHAT ABOUT YOU?

1. What is a **problem** you have?

   _____
   _____

2. Who is affected by this **problem** other than yourself?

   _____
   _____

3. What are the benefits of solving this **problem**?

   _____
   _____

4. What are the consequences if this **problem** is not solved?

   _____
   _____

5. What are the **causes of this problem**?

   _____
   _____

6. What are two possible **solutions** to the **problem**?

   _____
   _____

Kids Navigating Life - Level 3

7. What are the effects of the first **solution**?

    Positive: _____

    Negative: _____

8. What are the effects of the second **solution**?

    Positive: _____

    Negative: _____

9. Which **solution** do you think will be most successful?

    _____

    _____

Thinking Critically

TEST YOURSELF!

Post Test: Circle your answers and fill in the blanks to the questions.

1. What is a **solution**?
   A. An answer to a problem or an explanation
   B. Nose hair

2. What is an **outcome**?
   A. The end result after an action or inaction
   B. The sound a mad mouse would make

3. What does **decision making** mean?
   A. To work on making a decision based on all information
   B. To work on coming to a conclusion based on all information
   C. All of the above

4. What is an **origin**?
   A. Where something starts.
   B. The root of a problem or conflict.
   C. The source of the trouble.
   D. All of the above.

5. What do you need to find to solve a **problem**?
   A. The origin of the problem
   B. The origin of the conflict
   C. All of the above

6. How can you find an **origin** of a **problem** or **conflict**?
   A. Ask questions of others
   B. Talk about the problem with people involved
   C. Research books
   D. All of the above

Kids Navigating Life - Level 3

7. How do you determine what the **problem** is?
   A. Guess
   B. Gather information from people involved
   C. Talk to your pets
   D. All of the above

8. What is an **alternative solution**?
   A. A different solution than the one you came up with
   B. A different solution than the one you used
   C. All of the above

9. What does **win/win** mean?

   _____

   _____

   _____

10. What skill does it take to reach **win/win**?
    ❑ Conflict resolution or management
    ❑ Decision making
    ❑ Researching
    ❑ Negotiating
    ❑ Identifying my emotions

Advanced Question: How are conflict resolution and conflict management different from one another?

_____

_____

_____

_____

Thinking Critically

CONGRATULATIONS!

YOU DID IT! You now have the knowledge and have demonstrated some of the important skills you need to be able to solve problems and resolve or manage conflict successfully.

You also identified some emotions that can be part of these two skills. You not only identified the emotions you would feel but also important, those of others.

For extra credit answer these questions:

1. What skills do I need to spend more time on?
    - ❑ Problem solving
    - ❑ Conflict resolution or management
    - ❑ Decision making
    - ❑ Researching
    - ❑ Negotiating
    - ❑ Identifying my emotions

2. Who can I ask to help me practice these skills? _____
   _____

3. Which skills do I feel most confident about?
    - ❑ Problem solving
    - ❑ Conflict resolution or management
    - ❑ Decision making
    - ❑ Researching
    - ❑ Negotiating
    - ❑ Identifying my emotions

Keep going! There is so much to learn that will help make your life better!

You are doing great!

Kids Navigating Life - Level 3

Course 5

Gaining Social Skills

Skills

Social Interaction

Table Manners

Personal Grooming and Proper Clothing

Basic Courtesies

Learning Outcomes

Upon completing this course the student will be able to:

1. Define terms used when socially interacting

2. Identify opportunities to make a difference in a community

3. Identify foundations that give back to a community

4. Identify the benefits to self and others when paying it forward

5. Identify appropriate and inappropriate behaviors

Course Introduction

The student will become familiar with terms used in the skill area of social interaction. They will also identify resources available to help them determine what is appropriate behavior and attire for a given event or situation.

Social skills will be practiced and emotions associated with lack of knowledge, and inappropriate behavior of self and others will be identified.

Kids Navigating Life - Level 3

 **NEW WORDS!**

Social Interaction: Social interaction is how we get along with other people. Social skills help us to behave in a way that is acceptable in a civil society. Every day there are opportunities to interact socially with others. Think back to how many people you have already interacted with today. Most likely there were quite a few in a short period of time. Interacting well with others is important. Academic skills will take us so far. We need the social skills to get the rest of the way.

Table Manners: Table manners are how you should behave at the table when you are eating. These manners are very important. Using good table manners shows respect for people you are eating with. Using good table manners also gives you many opportunities which you may not otherwise be given.

Personal Grooming and Proper Clothing: Personal grooming is the tasks we perform every day to ensure we are clean and presentable. Proper clothing means selecting the appropriate clothes and shoes for an event.

Basic Courtesies: These are the skills that show you are patient, kind, and thoughtful in a civil society. There are many opportunities every day to practice these skills in our society. We can extend basic courtesies to all we meet whether it is wishing someone a good day or saying thank you.

Gaining Social Skills

DEFINE IT!

What does **appropriate** mean?
Appropriate means to be right or suitable for the purpose. Examples: being quiet in a library is **appropriate** or yelling at a football game is **appropriate**. Yelling in the library would not be appropriate.

What does **civil** mean?
Civil means a community of citizens who behave in a cultured, polite, and courteous manner. To be **civil** is to practice the etiquette and social behavior that is appropriate within a community such as a school or neighborhood. **Uncivilized** is to be rude, mean, and thoughtless.

What is a **community of citizens**?
A **community of citizens** is a group of people living and/or working together such as neighbors in a neighborhood community, teachers and students in a school community, or store owners in a shopping mall community.

What does **society** mean?
Society means all people belonging to a group.

What does **choice** mean?
Choice means the act of choosing or making a selection. It is an option or alternative.

What is an **opportunity**?
An **opportunity** is a combination of favorable circumstances. For example, if you finish your homework early and later a friend asks you to go to the basketball game. Because you finished your homework early, your parents give you permission to go. You gave yourself that opportunity by finishing your homework early.

What is **courtesy**?
Courtesy is behavior that is polite, helpful, and considerate. It can be an act or a remark or a gesture of goodwill.

Kids Navigating Life - Level 3

TEST YOURSELF

Pretest: Circle the correct answers and fill in the blanks to the questions.

1. What does **appropriate** mean?
    A. To be right or suitable for the purpose
    B. Yell in the library

2. What does **civil** mean?
    A. A community of citizens who behave in a cultured, polite, and courteous manner
    B. To practice the etiquette and social behavior that is appropriate within a community
    C. To be rude, mean, and thoughtless
    D. a and b

3. What is a **community of citizens**?
    A. A group of people living together such as neighbors
    B. A group of people working together such as teachers and students
    C. A group of store owners in a shopping mall
    D. All of the above

4. What does **society** mean?
    A. All people belonging to a group
    B. Old sandwich

5. What does **choice** mean?
    A. The act of choosing or making a selection
    B. An option or alternative
    C. All of the above

6. What is an **opportunity**?
    A combination of _____ circumstances

7. What is **courtesy**?
    Courtesy is a behavior that is _____, _____, and _____.

Gaining Social Skills

COURSE SCENARIO!

In each course of the workbook, you will read about a pretend situation, or scenario. These situations will give you a chance to apply the skills of the course as you are learning about them. As you read the scenario, think about your own life and if this has ever happened to you, then answer the questions at the end.

Dixon's behavior is not civil. It is uncivilized. He is rude, thoughtless, and mean. He pushes other kids out of line so he can be first. He makes fun of the other kids. He doesn't hold the door open for people behind him, and you never hear him say please and thank you. He wears clothes to school he is not supposed to wear, chews with his mouth open and talks when his mouth is full of food.

Trevor's behavior is civil. He is polite, courteous, and kind. He let Judy get in front of him in line because she was on crutches. He helped Matt with the science problem in class. He thanked Dixon's mom for giving him a ride to school. He always dresses according to school dress code and uses good table manners at the lunch table.

The principal needs a student representative to greet and give a tour of the school to a visiting professional football player. The student will need to attend the dinner planned for the football player. The principal is going to make a choice between Dixon and Trevor. Both Dixon and Trevor think this football player is the greatest football player of all time.

The principal chooses Trevor because he represents the school community and his behavior is appropriate. He is courteous, thoughtful, and kind.

MAKING IT REAL

1. Are you a good representative of your school community? Yes ❑ No ❑

2. If yes, why? _____
   _____

3. Why is Dixon's behavior considered **uncivilized**? _____
   _____
   _____

Kids Navigating Life - Level 3

4. Why is Trevor's behavior considered **civil**? _____

   _____

   _____

5. Who set himself up for the **opportunity** of being a school representative for the football player's visit? Dixon _____ Trevor _____

6. What did Trevor do to show he was deserving of the **opportunity**?

   _____

   _____

   _____

7. What **choices** can Dixon make now so he might be chosen next time?

   _____

   _____

   _____

8. Who could you ask for help if you needed to learn more about what clothing and behavior is appropriate and not appropriate for a given situation?

   _____

   _____

   _____

Gaining Social Skills

WHAT ABOUT YOU?

1. Would you consider yourself **civil** or **uncivilized** and why?
   _____
   _____

2. If you thought you could be more **civil** within your **community**, who could you go to in order to find out how?
   _____
   _____

3. Every action is a **choice**. What choices have you made today?
   _____
   _____

4. What is a possible **opportunity** available to you right now or in the near future?
   _____
   _____

5. How can you set yourself up to succeed in this **opportunity**?
   _____
   _____

6. Define **appropriate** and give an example:
   _____
   _____

Kids Navigating Life - Level 3

SCENARIO ACTIVITY PRACTICE!

Four Foundations

There are those in our community who create foundations to give back to society. Many do this because they feel the community has given so much to them.

A foundation is an organization created to assist others.

In this activity, you will identify four foundations, their founders, and what the foundations do to help others.

Founders can be sports figures, actors or actresses, community leaders, business owners, singers, musicians, and neighbors.

1.

Founder:	Occupation:
Name of Foundation:	
What does this foundation do?	

2.

Founder:	Occupation:
Name of Foundation:	
What does this foundation do?	

3.

Founder:	Occupation:
Name of Foundation:	
What does this foundation do?	

Gaining Social Skills

4.

Founder:	Occupation:
Name of Foundation:	
What does this foundation do?	

One TOUGH Question!

How do the founders you selected benefit from having these foundations?

1. _____

2. _____

3. _____

4. _____

Kids Navigating Life - Level 3

SHOW YOUR SKILLS!

The Orbs of Opportunity

The Orbs of Opportunity will show you how you can give back by *paying it forward*.

Paying it forward means to give by doing good things for other people. These people then will possibly be encouraged to do the same.

Every day we have many opportunities to *pay it forward* by being kind to others.

Think about the opportunities you have had today.

Examples of Social Skills
Being polite
Using good table manners
Holding door open for someone
Saying please and thank you
Being kind
Helping someone
Paying a compliment

What was the opportunity? _____
_____
_____

Which social skills did you use?
_____
_____
_____
_____

How did the person respond? _____
_____
_____

Would you do this again? If yes, why? _____
_____
_____

How did it benefit others? _____
_____
_____

How did it benefit you?
_____
_____
_____

Gaining Social Skills

WHAT ABOUT YOU?

Now that you've identified an opportunity you chose to act on, identify an opportunity you chose not to act on.

1. What was the **opportunity** you did not act on?

   _____

   _____

2. Why didn't you act on the **opportunity**?

   _____

   _____

3. What benefits did the person you would have helped miss out on?

   _____

   _____

4. What benefits did you miss out on?

   _____

5. How did it make you feel when you realized you missed out on the **opportunity** to help someone? _____

   _____

6. What would you do differently next time you came across the same or similar **opportunity**? _____

   _____

Kids Navigating Life - Level 3

TEST YOURSELF

Post Test: Circle the correct answers and fill in the blanks to the questions.

1. What does **appropriate** mean?
    A. To be right or suitable for the purpose
    B. Yell in the library

2. What does **civil** mean?
    A. A community of citizens who behave in a cultured, polite, and courteous manner
    B. To practice the etiquette and social behavior that is appropriate within a community
    C. To be rude, mean, and thoughtless
    D. a and b

3. What is a **community of citizens**?
    A. A group of people living together such as neighbors
    B. A group of people working together such as teachers and students
    C. A group of store owners in a shopping mall
    D. All of the above

4. What does **society** mean?
    A. All people belonging to a group
    B. Old sandwich

5. What does **choice** mean?
    A. The act of choosing or making a selection
    B. An option or alternative
    C. All of the above

6. What is an **opportunity**?
    A combination of _____ circumstances

7. What is **courtesy**?
    Courtesy is a behavior that is _____, _____, and _____.

Gaining Social Skills

CONGRATULATIONS!

YOU DID IT! You have just learned some social skills you need to succeed. You identified foundations that give back to their community and what it means to be a valued member of a community. You identified opportunities to use social skills. You also wrote down an opportunity you chose to miss out on and what you will do differently next time.

For extra credit answer these questions:

Which skills do I still need to practice?
- ❏ Social interaction
- ❏ Table manners
- ❏ Personal grooming and proper clothing
- ❏ Basic courtesies
- ❏ Identifying my emotions

Who can I ask to help me practice these skills?

_____

_____

Which skills am I really good at?
- ❏ Social interaction
- ❏ Table manners
- ❏ Personal grooming and proper clothing
- ❏ Basic courtesies
- ❏ Identifying my emotions

Keep going! There is so much to learn that will help make your life better!

You are doing great!

Kids Navigating Life - Level 3

Course 6

Planning a Project

Skills
Time Management
Organization
Prioritizing
Adaptabilility
Teamwork
Evaluation

Learning Outcomes

Upon completing this course the student will be able to:

1. Define evaluate

2. Define outcome

3. Prioritize steps to complete a task or goal

4. Utilize steps necessary to evaluate a project

5. Identify what needs to be done if the results don't match the desired outcome

Course Introduction

The student will become familiar with terms used in the skill areas of project planning such as time management, planning, organizing, prioritizing, teamwork, and evaluation. They will identify steps it takes to complete a task in order of priority. The student will be introduced to the concepts of outcome and evaluation.

Kids Navigating Life - Level 3

 **NEW WORDS!**

Time Management: Time management is how you use your time to complete a project in the time allowed.

Project: A project is a task. For example, your project might be to make your lunch.

Plan: A plan is something you follow to complete a project. You might create a plan yourself. For example, you might make a plan to finish all of your homework by 7:00 PM.

Organize: To organize means to arrange. For example, you might organize your books or music alphabetically.

Prioritize: To prioritize means to identify what you need to do first.

Adaptable: To be adaptable means to be flexible and accept changes or new ideas.

Teamwork: Teamwork means to cooperate with other people to reach a goal or to complete a project.

Evaluate: To evaluate means to assess or to determine if the result you wanted is the result you got.

Outcome: An outcome is the consequence or the result.

Planning a Project

 **DEFINE IT!**

What is **time management**?
>**Time management** is how you use your time to complete a project in the time allowed.

What is a **project**?
>A **project** is a task.

What is a **plan**?
>A **plan** is something you follow to complete a project.

What does it mean to **organize**?
>To **organize** means to arrange.

What does it mean to **prioritize**?
>To **prioritize** means to identify what you need to do first.

What does it mean to be **adaptable**?
>To be **adaptable** means to be flexible and accept changes or new ideas.

What is **teamwork**?
>**Teamwork** means to cooperate with other people to reach a goal or to complete a project.

What does it mean to **evaluate**?
>To **evaluate** means to determine if the result you wanted is the result you got.

What is an **outcome**?
>An **outcome** is the consequence or the result.

Kids Navigating Life - Level 3

 **TEST YOURSELF!**

Pretest: Circle the correct answers.

1. What is **time management**?
    A. How you use your time to complete a project in the time allowed
    B. How you don't figure time into a project
    C. All of the above

2. What is a **plan**?
    A. Instructions you follow to complete a project
    B. A map or a strategy to follow to complete a project
    C. All of the above

3. What does it mean to **organize**?
    A. To arrange
    B. To categorize
    C. To rename
    D. All of the above

4. What is a **project**?
    A. A task
    B. Making an effort
    C. All of the above

5. What does it mean to **prioritize**?
    A. To identify what you need to do first
    B. To identify what is most important
    C. All of the above

Planning a Project

6. What does it mean to be **adaptable**?
    A. To be flexible and accept changes or new ideas
    B. To disagree with others
    C. All of the above

7. What does **teamwork** mean?
    A. To cooperate with other people to reach a goal
    B. To work by yourself
    C. All of the above

8. What does **evaluate** mean?
    A. To determine if the result you wanted is the result you got
    B. To not care about the result
    C. All of the above

9. What is an **outcome**?
    A. A result or a consequence
    B. How you get to the end result
    C. All of the above

Kids Navigating Life - Level 3

COURSE SCENARIO!

In each course of this workbook is a pretend situation, or a scenario. Read the story and answer the questions. Think about if this has ever happened to you.

Trish, Rick, Robbie, and Stephanie are working together as a team on their geography project. The project is they have to make a topographical map of their state. They all want to get an A.

Trish's strength is that she is very good at research. Her part in the project is to research the different elevations in the state and the state "fun facts," then she is to give them to her teammates.

Robbie's strength is he has a library of geography books with maps at home. He has offered to help Trish with research using the books. Robbie will give Trish the information he finds.

Stephanie's strength is that she is creative and enjoys working on projects. She's offered to create the topographical map of the state using the information from Trish and Robbie.

Rick's strength is that he is amazing at computer graphics. His part in the project is to create a paper with all of the important state information such as the state flower, state bird, and different elevations they use in their project. The team will include that information in their presentation to the class.

In order to complete this project on time, each member of the team is going to have to be responsible for his or her own part in the project. The team has two weeks to finish the project before they have to present it to the class.

MAKING IT REAL

1. Have you worked on a project with other people? Yes ❑ No ❑

2. What was your **project**? _____

_____

3. What is the **project** the team in the scenario is working on? _____

_____

_____

Planning a Project

4. What do they have to **organize** before they begin? _____
_____

5. What is the time allowed to complete the **project**? _____
_____

6. Why do they have to use **time management**? _____
_____

7. What strengths does Trish have? _____
_____

8. What strengths does Rick have? _____
_____

9. What strengths does Robbie have? _____
_____

10. What strengths does Stephanie have? _____
_____

11. What is the **outcome** each team member wants? _____
_____

12. In order to complete the **project**, what is each team member responsible for?

    Trish: _____

    Robbie: _____

    Rick: _____

    Stephanie: _____

Kids Navigating Life - Level 3

WHAT ABOUT YOU?

1. What is a **project** you are working on right now or want to work on? _____
   _____
   _____

2. What is the **outcome** you want to achieve? _____
   _____

3. What is the **plan** you will use to reach that outcome? _____
   _____
   _____

4. Have you **prioritized** what you need to do first? Yes ❏ No ❏

   What is the first **priority**? _____

   What is the second **priority**? _____

5. What supplies will you need to do your **project**? _____
   _____
   _____

6. What will you need to **organize** before you begin? _____
   _____
   _____

Planning a Project

7. How much time do you have to work on your **project**? _____
   _____

8. How will you get your **project** done on time? _____
   _____
   _____

9. Have there been new ideas or changes to the **project** since you started?

   Yes ❑   No ❑

   If yes, what are they? _____
   _____

10. Are you able to be **adaptable** or flexible to the new ideas or changes?

    Yes ❑   No ❑   If yes, how? _____
    _____

    If no, why not? _____
    _____

11. Are you using **teamwork** to work on or to complete this project? Yes ❑   No ❑

    If yes, how many people are on the team? _____

    What is your role on the team? _____

    If no, would having a team help you to finish the project more quickly?

    Yes ❑   No ❑

12. How will you **evaluate** to determine if you got the result you wanted at the end of your **project**? _____
    _____
    _____

Kids Navigating Life - Level 3

SCENARIO ACTIVITY PRACTICE!

This is a project planning activity. Remember Trish, Robbie, Rick, and Stephanie? Their team project is to work as a team to create a topographical map of their state. Their desired outcome is for each team member to get an A.

Complete the following task list for one of the team members. You decide who you want to complete it for.

Use this form to write down each of the steps your team member needs to complete in the order necessary to complete the project. Write down how much time you will give your team member to complete each step in the Time Allowed section. In order to finish on time, it's important to know how much time it will take to complete each step.

TASK LIST

Team Member Name: _____

Project: __Create a topographical map of the state__

Responsible For: _____

_____

Project Time Allowed: __Two weeks__

Steps Needed to Complete the Project: Time Allowed:

Step 1. _____   _____

Step 2. _____   _____

Step 3. _____   _____

Step 4. _____   _____

Step 5. _____   _____

Step 6. _____   _____

Planning a Project

Now that you've completed the task list, use that task list to determine what supplies your person (Rick, Trish, Robbie, or Stephanie) will need.

Complete the following supply list for the teammate you chose for the task list.

SUPPLY LIST

Team Member Name: _____

Project: __Create a topographical map of the state__

Responsible For: _____
_____

Project Time Allowed: __Two weeks__

Supplies Needed: (Put a check mark in the box when you get each item.)

☐ _____

☐ _____

☐ _____

☐ _____

☐ _____

☐ _____

Great job! You have just learned about two very important pieces of project planning. You can use these lists every time you have a project. Use the task list to keep you on track with time, and use the supply list to organize the supplies you will need to complete the project.

Another very important piece in project planning is the contact list of all of your teammates. This helps each member communicate with the others.

Name: _____ Home phone: _____

Email Address: _____ Cell phone: _____

Class Schedule: _____

Kids Navigating Life - Level 3

SHOW YOUR SKILLS!

To complete a successful project, you want to make sure the people on your team are using their strengths. For example, let's say you were working on a project and one of the tasks was to present the project in front of the class and talk about it. If you are good at speaking in front of the class, you might offer to do that part of the project. If your teammate does not like speaking in front of the class but has good computer skills, your teammate might offer to write the paper instead of speak in front of the class.

So, here is your opportunity to identify your strengths. List as many as you can. You might even ask your parents, friends, or teacher to tell you what they think your strengths are.

I am good at:

_____

_____

_____

I like these things about myself:

_____

_____

_____

People say I'm good at:

_____

_____

_____

Planning a Project

WHAT ABOUT YOU?

Evaluation Station

This activity is about evaluating the outcome of a project to make sure you have reached the results you want or someone else requires of you (like a teacher).

Follow the instructions listed in The Plan.

The Plan
Step 1: Draw a star in the upper right-hand corner of this box.
Step 2: Underline the words "Evaluation Station" above this box.
Step 3: Write, "Planning Your Project" in the lower left-hand corner of this box.
Step 4: Draw a squiggly line above the words "What About You" on the top of this page.

Compare the image below with what you've done above to determine if you got the results required by The Plan.

Let's Evaluate! Check the boxes if your outcome is the same as the one on the image.

❏ Star in the same location
❏ "Evaluation Station" underlined
❏ "Planning Your Project" written in the same location
❏ Squiggly line above "What About You"

How was your evaluation? Did you check all four boxes? If not, you might have to go back and follow the instructions again to see what you missed.

You've now evaluated a project. Another tool you can use in Project Planning!

Kids Navigating Life - Level 3

 **TEST YOURSELF!**

Post Test: Circle the correct answers.

1. What is **time management**?
    A. How you use your time to complete a project in the time allowed
    B. How you don't figure time into a project
    C. All of the above

2. What is a **plan**?
    A. Instructions you follow to complete a project
    B. A map or a strategy to follow to complete a project
    C. All of the above

3. What does it mean to **organize**?
    A. To arrange
    B. To categorize
    C. To rename
    D. All of the above

4. What is a **project**?
    A. A task
    B. Making an effort
    C. All of the above

5. What does it mean to **prioritize**?
    A. To identify what you need to do first
    B. To identify what is most important
    C. All of the above

Planning a Project

6. What does it mean to be **adaptable**?
    A. To be flexible and accept changes or new ideas
    B. To disagree with others
    C. All of the above

7. What does **teamwork** mean?
    A. To cooperate with other people to reach a goal
    B. To work by yourself
    C. All of the above

8. What does **evaluate** mean?
    A. To determine if the result you wanted is the result you got
    B. To not care about the result
    C. All of the above

9. What is an **outcome**?
    A. A result or a consequence
    B. How you get to the end result
    C. All of the above

Kids Navigating Life - Level 3

CONGRATULATIONS!

YOU DID IT! You have just practiced some project planning skills. Great job! You identified how Trish, Rick, Robbie and Stephanie worked as a team to complete their project. You prioritized by putting in order the steps you take to complete a project. You completed a task list and a supply list. You identified your strengths according to you and others. You also learned about teamwork skills and how to evaluate a completed project for desired outcome.

For extra credit answer these questions:

Which skills do I still need to practice?
- ❏ Time management
- ❏ Planning
- ❏ Organizing
- ❏ Prioritizing
- ❏ Adaptability
- ❏ Teamwork
- ❏ Evaluation

Who can I ask to help me practice these skills?

_____

_____

Which skills am I really good at?
- ❏ Time management
- ❏ Planning
- ❏ Organizing
- ❏ Prioritizing
- ❏ Adaptability
- ❏ Teamwork
- ❏ Evaluation

Keep going! There is so much to learn that will help make your life better!

You are doing great!

Course 7

Making a Difference

Skills
Commitment
Leadership
Diversity
Support of Others
Service to Others

Learning Outcomes

Upon completing this course the student will be able to:

1. Identify qualities of a leader

2. Discuss their personal biases and how they may affect their judgment

3. Recognize the commonalities among a diverse group

4. Identify how they can be supportive of others

5. Identify how they can provide service to others

Course Introduction

The student will become familiar with terms used in the skill areas of making a difference such as leadership, commitment, diversity, and support of and service to others. They will identify ways they can work within diversity and support and serve others. They will also identify their own personal biases and why and how those biases are impacting their judgment.

Kids Navigating Life - Level 3

 **NEW WORDS!**

Leadership: Leadership means to lead. Example, you might run for president of your student body association. A leader is someone who chooses to do the right thing instead of following others who are doing something that is wrong.

Commitment: A commitment is a pledge to do something. Example, you might make a commitment to the student body to work to make positive change.

Diversity: Diversity means to include and work with people who are different from you. Example, you might be a lab partner in science class with someone of a different race, background, skill set, or disability.

Support of Others: To show support of others means to give help or assist in some way to someone who needs it. Example, you might help your friend with his or her homework.

Service to Others: To show service to others means to do something for someone who needs it. Example, you might carry your friend's books to his or her locker because your friend is on crutches.

Personal Biases: Personal biases are personal judgments of someone based on your prior experience, your knowledge or ignorance, and/or your environment. For example, you may have a personal bias against people who exercise because you don't like to exercise. Your personal bias may show itself outwardly by you having a negative attitude or making negative comments towards someone who exercises.

Making a Difference

 **DEFINE IT!**

What is **leadership**?
    Leadership means to lead.

What is **commitment**?
    A **commitment** is a pledge or agreement to do something in the future.

What is **diversity**?
    Diversity is the condition of being different. It also means to include and work with people who are different from you.

What does it mean to show **support of others**?
    To show **support of others** means to give help or assist in some way to someone who needs it.

What does it mean to show **service to others**?
    To show **service to others** means to offer to or do something for someone who needs it.

What are **personal biases**?
    Personal biases are personal judgments of someone based on your prior experience, your knowledge or ignorance, and/or your environment.

Kids Navigating Life - Level 3

TEST YOURSELF!

Pretest: Circle the correct answers.

1. What is **leadership**?
    A. To lead
    B. To follow
    C. All of the above

2. What is **commitment**?
    A. Not taking responsibility
    B. An agreement to do something in the future
    C. All of the above

3. What is **diversity**?
    A. The condition of being different
    B. The condition of being the same as others
    C. All of the above

4. What does it mean to show **support of others**?
    A. To give help in some way to someone who needs it
    B. To ignore someone in need
    C. All of the above

5. What does it mean to show **service to others**?
    A. To do something for someone who needs it
    B. To lack compassion for others
    C. All of the above

6. What are **personal biases**?
    A. Personal judgments based on prior experience
    B. Personal judgments based on ignorance
    C. Personal judgments based on environment
    D. All of the above

Making a Difference

COURSE SCENARIO!

In each course of this workbook is a pretend situation, or a scenario. Read the story and answer the questions. Think about if this has ever happened to you.

Clive and Stacy are both running for student body president. This position would require the candidate to have leadership qualities.

Clive plays soccer and basketball and is an "A" student.

Stacy plays volleyball and tennis and is also an "A" student.

Clive is friendly, outgoing, honest, and has a great attitude.

Stacy is kind, social, trustworthy, and has a positive attitude.

Clive is a great problem solver and decision maker.

Stacy is great at solving problems and making decisions.

Clive's parents are divorced.

Stacy's parents are married.

MAKING IT REAL

1. Would you vote for Clive or Stacy for the position of student body president?

   _____

   Why? _____

   _____

   _____

2. How are Clive and Stacy alike? _____

   _____

   _____

Kids Navigating Life - Level 3

3. How are Clive and Stacy different? _____
   _____
   _____

4. What character traits or qualities does Clive have that would benefit him as a **leader**?
   _____
   _____

5. What character traits does Stacy have that would benefit her as a **leader**?
   _____
   _____

6. Would you choose Clive over Stacy because he plays soccer and basketball?
   Yes ❏ No ❏

   Why? _____

7. Would you choose Stacy over Clive because she plays volleyball and tennis?
   Yes ❏ No ❏

   Why? _____

8. Would you choose Clive over Stacy because he's a male? Yes ❏ No ❏

   Why? _____

9. Would you choose Stacy over Clive because she's a female? Yes ❏ No ❏

   Why? _____

10. Would you choose Clive over Stacy because his parents are divorced?
    Yes ❏ No ❏

    Why? _____

11. Would you choose Stacy over Clive because her parents are married?

    Yes ❏ No ❏

    Why? _____

Making a Difference

Everyone has **personal biases**. It's what you do with your biases that is important. The first step is to recognize you have them.

The second step is to identify the personal biases you have.

Then, reflect on your experience and ask people you respect and trust whether your biases are supporting you and others or hurting you and others.

Think about your own **personal biases**. Did those biases impact your judgment of Clive or Stacy? Yes ❑ No ❑

If yes, how? _____

_____

_____

Kids Navigating Life - Level 3

WHAT ABOUT YOU?

1. Do you have **personal biases**? Yes ☐ No ☐

   What are those **personal biases**? _____
   _____

2. How can you learn if your **biases** are supporting you and others or hurting you and others? _____
   _____

3. Who are some respected and trusted people you can talk to about your **personal biases**? _____
   _____

4. Is there **diversity** in your home? Yes ☐ No ☐

5. Is there **diversity** in your classroom at school? Yes ☐ No ☐

6. Is there **diversity** in your neighborhood? Yes ☐ No ☐

7. Have you ever shown **support of others** to someone different than yourself? Yes ☐ No ☐

   How did you show that **support of others**? _____
   _____

8. Have you ever shown **service to others** to someone different than yourself? Yes ☐ No ☐

   How did you show that **service to others**? _____
   _____

Making a Difference

SCENARIO ACTIVITY PRACTICE!

Commonalities Among Diversity

Here is a list of information about five people. These five people are very different. They also share many commonalities. Using the information and the graph on the following page, you will place an X in each area that applies for each of the five people.

We have done the first one for you.

1. Leela, Brenda, Tino, Raj, and May all live on Fairway Avenue.
2. Leela, Brenda, Tino, Raj, and May are all 12 years old.
3. Leela is African American.
4. Brenda is Norwegian.
5. Tino is Mexican.
6. Raj is East Indian.
7. May is Asian.
8. Leela, Brenda, May, Tino, and Raj are all members of the human race.
9. Leela, Brenda, and May are girls.
10. Tino and Raj are boys.
11. Brenda and Tino wear glasses.
12. Leela, May, and Raj wear contact lenses.
13. Leela, Tino, Raj, and May all have dark hair.
14. Tino's, Raj's, Leela's, Brenda's, and May's grandparents were born outside the United States.
15. Tino, Raj, Leela, Brenda, and May were born in the United States.
16. Brenda has dyslexia. Raj has difficulty with reading English.
17. May's and Brenda's last names are difficult to pronounce for English speaking people.
18. Tino broke his arm riding his bike and is in a cast.
19. Brenda broke her leg riding a horse.

Kids Navigating Life - Level 3

Graph for Commonalities Among Diversity Activity

	Leela	Brenda	Tino	Raj	May
Live on Fairway Ave.	X	X	X	X	X
12 years old					
African American					
Norwegian					
Mexican					
East Indian					
Asian					
Human Race					
Girls					
Boys					
Glasses or contact lenses					
Dark hair					
Grandparents born outside the USA					
Born in the USA					
Dyslexia or difficulty reading					
Last names difficult to pronounce					
Broken limb					

Making a Difference

SHOW YOUR SKILLS!

What Would You Do?

In the previous activity, you saw how five very different people can have many things in common. We all share at least one commonality—that of being part of the human race. This connects all people. As you do this next activity, think about how we are all connected.

Follow the path of support and service. Read each story in the box and check off what you would do to show support of others or service to others. There can be more than one answer.

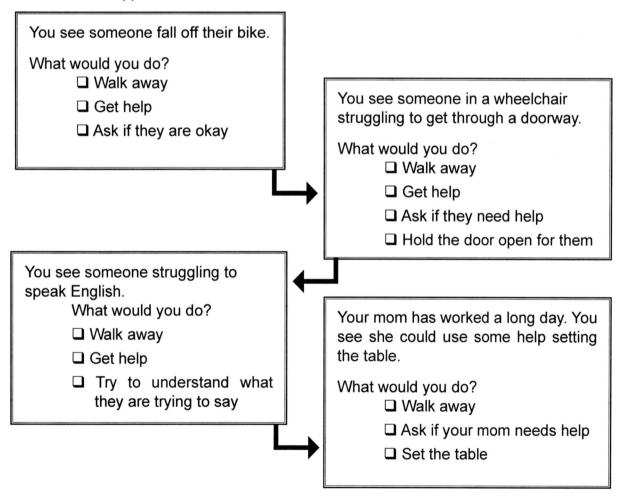

Kids Navigating Life - Level 3

WHAT ABOUT YOU?

In the last activity, you checked off what you would do in each scenario. For this activity, we're going to have you look at your reasons for checking those boxes and identifying what you might do differently next time.

1. You see someone fall off a bike.
   What did you check? ❏ Walk away ❏ Get help ❏ Ask if the person is okay
   How did that choice benefit you? _____

   _____

   How did that choice benefit the other person? _____

   _____

   Why did you make that choice? _____

   _____

   Would you choose to do something different next time? Yes ❏ No ❏
   If so, what would that be? _____
   Why? _____

2. You see someone in a wheelchair struggling to get through a doorway.
   What did you check? ❏ Walk away ❏ Get help ❏ Ask if the person is okay
   ❏ Hold the door open for the person
   How did that choice benefit you? _____

   _____

   How did that choice benefit the other person? _____

   _____

   Why did you make that choice? _____

   _____

Making a Difference

Would you choose to do something different next time? Yes ❑ No ❑
If so, what would that be? _____
Why? _____

3. You see someone struggling to speak English.
   What did you check? ❑ Walk away ❑ Get help ❑ Ask if the person is okay ❑ Try to understand what the person is trying to say
   How did that choice benefit you? _____
   _____

   How did that choice benefit the other person? _____
   _____

   Why did you make that choice? _____
   _____

   Would you choose to do something different next time? Yes ❑ No ❑
   If so, what would that be? _____
   Why? _____

4. Your mom has worked a long day. You see she could use some help setting the table.
   What did you check? ❑ Walk away ❑ Ask if your mom needs help ❑ Set the table
   How did that choice benefit you? _____
   _____

   How did that choice benefit the other person? _____
   _____

   Why did you make that choice? _____
   _____

   Would you choose to do something different next time? Yes ❑ No ❑
   If so, what would that be? _____
   Why? _____

Kids Navigating Life - Level 3

 **TEST YOURSELF!**

Post Test: Circle your answers.

1. What is **leadership**?
    A. To lead
    B. To follow
    C. All of the above

2. What is **commitment**?
    A. Not taking responsibility
    B. An agreement to do something in the future
    C. All of the above

3. What is **diversity**?
    A. The condition of being different
    B. The condition of being the same as others
    C. All of the above

4. What does it mean to show **support of others**?
    A. To give help in some way to someone who needs it
    B. To ignore someone in need
    C. All of the above

5. What does it mean to show **service to others**?
    A. To do something for someone who needs it
    B. To lack compassion for others
    C. All of the above

6. What are **personal biases**?
    A. Personal judgments based on prior experience
    B. Personal judgments based on ignorance
    C. Personal judgments based on environment
    D. All of the above

Making a Difference

CONGRATULATIONS!

YOU DID IT! You have just learned some skills you would use to make a difference. Great job! You worked with diversity and identified commonalities and differences, as well as character traits or qualities of a leader. You learned about some qualities you look for in a leader. You also identified your own personal biases. How those biases might support you and others or hurt you and others. You identified persons you can talk to about your personal biases.

For extra credit answer these questions:

Which skills do I still need to practice?
- ❑ Commitment
- ❑ Leadership
- ❑ Diversity
- ❑ Support of Others
- ❑ Service to Others

Who can I ask to help me practice these skills?

_____

_____

Which skills am I really good at?
- ❑ Commitment
- ❑ Leadership
- ❑ Diversity
- ❑ Support of Others
- ❑ Service to Others

Certificate of Achievement

You've done it!

Name _____

You've successfully navigated through this whole workbook and learned so many skills that will help you to have a better life! Keep practicing what you have learned and ask questions if you don't understand. These skills are the secret to success!

Great job!

_____

Teacher/Parent/Counselor/Mentor

Date_____

Kids Navigating Life

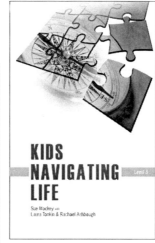

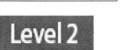

To order copies of **Kids Navigating Life**
(Retail $11.95)

1 – 9	$ 10.95	ea.
10 – 24	$ 9.95	ea.
25 – 99	$ 8.95	ea.
100+	$ 7.95	ea.

Larger bulk quantity pricing available on request

Other books and workbooks brought to you by The Mackey Group

To order copies of **Women Navigating Adversity: The Courage They Didn't Know They Had** by Sue Mackey (Retail $12.00)
- 1 – 9 $10.00 ea.
- 10 – 24 $ 8.50 ea.
- 25 – 99 $ 7.00 ea.
- 100+ $ 6.00 ea.

To order copies of **Living Well, Working Smart: Soft Skills for Success** by Sue Mackey and Laura Tonkin (Retail $17.95)
- 1 – 9 $14.00 ea.
- 10 – 24 $12.50 ea.
- 25 – 99 $11.00 ea.
- 100+ $10.00 ea.

To order copies of **Twelve Pillars of Success Workbook** by Sue Mackey and Laura Tonkin and **Twelve Pillars** by Jim Rohn and Chris Widener (Retail set price $25.90)
- 1 – 9 $18.00 ea. set
- 10 – 24 $15.00 ea. set
- 25 – 99 $12.00 ea. set

To order copies of **The Honey-Do Survival Guide** by Sue Mackey and Laura Tonkin (Retail $15.00)
- 1 – 9 $11.00 ea.
- 10 – 24 $ 9.50 ea.
- 25 – 99 $ 8.00 ea.
- 100+ $ 7.00 ea.

Larger bulk ordering available upon request.

Standard Shipping & Handling

For Orders	Please Add
Up to $24.99	$4.95
$25 to $74.99	$6.50
$75 to $149.99	$7.95
$150 to $299.99	$9.50
$300 and Over	3%

Applies to US orders sent USPS Ground. Call for quotes on International and overnight shipping.

Phone Orders:
425-391-8776

Email Orders:
info@mackeygroup.com

Mail Orders:
The Mackey Group
PO Box 1247
Issaquah, WA 98027

Web Orders:
www.mackeygroup.com

TITLE	QUANTITY	UNIT PRICE	TOTAL
		SUBTOTAL	
Washington residents please add 9% sales tax			
		TOTAL	

Payment—please circle one: Check   VISA   MasterCard

Name: _____

Phone: ( ) _____

Address: _____

City/State/Zip: _____

Credit Card Number: _____

Expiration Date: _____

Signature: _____